Sticky As

Sticky Assessment: Classroom Strategies to Amplify Student Learning is a straightforward guide to assessment, designed to demystify assessment and to give teachers the tools they need to become better assessors. Translating the latest research into a concise and practical volume, this book helps teachers to monitor student learning, make assessment engaging and meaningful for students, and to use assessment that improves rather than merely measures learning outcomes. With examples from classroom teachers and exercises designed to help teachers think through their processes, this book will be an invaluable and lasting resource for classroom teachers.

Laura Greenstein has been an educator for over 30 years, serving as a teacher, department chair, and school leader in multiple grades and subjects. She teaches Human Development at the University of Connecticut. She also teaches graduate-level courses in Measurement, Assessment, and Evaluation, Portfolio Design, and Teaching, Learning, and Assessing with Technology at the University of New Haven. She is the founder of assessmentnetwork.net.

Sticky Assessment

Classroom Strategies to Amplify Student Learning

Laura Greenstein

Routledge
Taylor & Francis Group

NEW YORK AND LONDON

First published 2016
by Routledge
711 Third Avenue, New York, NY 10017

and by Routledge
2 Park Square, Milton Park, Abingdon, Oxon, OX14 4RN

Routledge is an imprint of the Taylor & Francis Group, an informa business

Library of Congress Cataloging-in-Publication Data
Names: Greenstein, Laura, author.
Title: Sticky assessment : classroom strategies to amplify student
learning / Laura Greenstein.
Description: New York, NY : Routledge, 2016. |
Includes bibliographical references and indexes.
Identifiers: LCCN 2015047808 | ISBN 9781138640900 (hardback) |
ISBN 9781138640917 (pbk.) | ISBN 9781315630885 (ebook)
Subjects: LCSH: Educational tests and measurements. |
Students—Rating of. | Effective teaching.
Classification: LCC LB3051 .G718 2016 | DDC 371.26—dc23
LC record available at http://lccn.loc.gov/2015047808

ISBN: 978-1-138-64090-0 (hbk)
ISBN: 978-1-138-64091-7 (pbk)
ISBN: 978-1-315-63088-5 (ebk)

Typeset in Palatino
by Florence Production Ltd, Stoodleigh, Devon

Dedicated to Sloane
And all her tomorrows

Contents

Illustrations

Figures

Tables

Preface

Do you really need to read another book on assessment? More than likely, you have read many books on this topic. Yet, from each one I read I take away a useful idea, concept, or strategy. For example, I learned from Dylan Wiliam (2011) that "what seems like a misconception is often, and perhaps usually, a perfectly good conception in the wrong place" (p. 74). John Hattie (2011) reminded me of the importance of knowing where each student begins and where that student is in their individual journey toward meeting the criteria of the lesson or unit. Pulling those ideas together, Carol Tomlinson and Tonya Moon (2013) support the value of "thinking about assessment in a differentiated classroom in terms of when it should occur, what should be assessed, and why assessment might be used" (p. 19). I would be pleased if you too find a new idea, provocative concept, or practical strategy to borrow from this book.

There is an abundance of well-marketed promotional materials urging us to purchase tests, data management programs, and assessment systems. At the same time there is a scarcity of information on verified assessment practices in classrooms and schools. Craig Mertler (2009), found that "teachers in the United States do not feel adequately prepared to assess their students' performance" (p. 101). This can be partly attributed to Lorrie Shepard's (2000) view that most "researchers do not assign a significant role to assessment as part of the learning process" (p. 12).

But this is changing and more research is now available on effective classroom practices. Greenberg and Walsh (2012) note that "the use of frequent assessments is a hallmark of the teaching profession in countries whose students outperform our own" (p. 2). While, at the same time, they note little has changed in the emphasis on formative assessment in pre-service and in-service learning in the United States and other countries.

Assessments that consistently rise to the top are those that are closely matched to learning outcomes, are informative for teachers and learners, utilize multiple strategies, engage learners, emphasize progress over final scores, and are balanced and fair. Assessment at its best is an ongoing process that is embedded throughout teaching and learning.

Why this Book is Important

In the words of James McMillan (2000), "What is most essential about assessment is understanding fundamental principles that can be used to enhance student learning and teacher effectiveness."

It makes me wonder, if we have all this information about assessment, why teachers don't use it. In workshops, they tell me that they are given assessments to administer to their students at predetermined times. At the same time they are urged to be better assessors, to accurately monitor student learning, to foster learners as assessors, to assess higher and deeper learning, and to use assessment to improve rather than merely measure learning outcomes.

What this Book is About

What you will find is a straightforward guide to best practice in assessment that is built on decades of research. What we now know is that teachers make a very big difference.

1. Among school-related factors, teachers have the greatest influence on student achievement (Killian, 2015) but there are a range of factors that influence teacher quality and effectiveness.
2. The most effective teachers continually engage and monitor students (Rand, 2012).
3. There are significant benefits of routinely using assessments to adjust instruction and achieve maximum performance (Black et al., 2002).
4. Among teachers, assessment is the least understood aspect of their work (Mertler, 2009).

The purpose of this book is to synthesize, in a user-friendly way, what is currently known about quality assessment: To explain it clearly, provide examples, and offer opportunities for practice. In it you will find a range of assessment strategies from selected choice to peer review of performances. The method is not most important; what matters is the purpose, placement, and process. This means starting with assessment in mind. As soon as the student learning targets and outcomes are identified, consider how they will be assessed. Make use of the data generated by pre-assessments and routine check-ins. If you are teaching about Shakespeare decide whether a selected choice test is your best option or would it be more meaningful to select a contemporary issue and have students write/perform a play about it in iambic pentameter. In science, do you want students to explain climate change or advocate for a response (or not responding) to climate change. Then, in reverse, purposefully plan learning and embed assessments based on intended learning targets.

Room to Grow

When I started teaching I knew little about assessment other than my own experience with selected choice and essay tests that I had taken as a student. Over time, I began to realize that when it came to assigning final grades, I was rather random in my approach. If a student seemed to have a different learning style or pace, I used the same assessment as everyone else to calculate a final score. Gradually I began to recognize that each learner has unique strengths and each learns differently, at different speeds, depths, and abilities to apply it. Learning is about making connections rather than memorizing unrelated vocabulary words or irrelevant (at least in the moment) facts. Assessment is more than determining a final score. It is about considering growth, providing multiple opportunities to show it, and engaging learners in the process.

What this Book is Not About

Over the decades, belief and practice about school design, instructional strategies, and standardized tests have come and gone.

From the experiments in the open classroom, to whole language, and unschooling we have learned about what doesn't work. The idea that we can evaluate teachers by their students' standardized test scores has proven fallible. So this book will not be about those topics. Nor is it intended to be read as a novel, but rather to be used as a reference and guide for implementing best practice.

How to Use the Ideas in the Book

Like a pocket dictionary, refer to this book regularly. Use it when you are not sure about how to adapt an assessment for a specific student or when you need help ensuring that your assessments align with your learning objectives, or to put some of the heavy lifting of assessment on the shoulders of the learners. You will find many strategies and examples of teachers in action as they use multiple strategies for varied purposes.

The book will encourage you to take a look at your own beliefs and practices about assessment and consider how that translates into practice. Think about your own experiences with assessment. Can you recall some really scary ones that made you feel incompetent or others that affirmed your skills and knowledge?

Before you begin, take a moment to reflect on your current beliefs and practices. Then write a note to yourself on each of these prompts. Come back later to see what's changed.

1. What are your beliefs about the purpose of assessment? Why do you assess?
2. When do you assess? At what point in teaching, how frequently?
3. How do you assess? What purposeful strategies do you use?
4. How do you engage learners in assessment? How are they the assessors in your classroom?
5. How do you respond to assessment data and information? What are some different ways that you use the data?
6. What questions will you be looking for answers to as you read this book?

Acknowledgments

There are countless people who made this book possible and I owe all of them my highest regard and deepest appreciation. As I tell my students, when you drop a pebble in the pond you never know how far and to whom those ripples will travel. It is those ripples that make all the difference in our lives.

I have had the privilege of working with many remarkable teachers, too many to list individually without inadvertently leaving someone out, but they each touched me, informed my beliefs, and guided my practice and I thank them all.

There have been many educational leaders who have facilitated my work, especially Ralph Jasparro at Johnson and Wales University and Charley Mojkowski at the Big Picture Schools. I also thank those school leaders who prodded me to dig deeper, question further, and shout out about the importance of quality assessment: Fred Chapman, Dave Erwin, Jim Lombardo, Mary Broderick, Nancy Niemi, and more.

And those professionals and practitioners who believe in the power of sticky assessment especially James McMillan (who reviewed this book in its early stages), Linda Darling-Hammond, John Hattie, Karin Hess, Dylan Wiliam, Heidi Andrade, Doug Fisher and Nancy Frey, and many others cited in the reference section.

Also, the many extraordinary people I've met through my publishing and consulting. Especially the fine folks at Routledge including Rebecca Novack and Matt Friberg who were consistently engaged and responsive, and the reviewers who were powerful advocates for its publication. And to the editors at Taylor and Francis.

At the very top of my personal list, I am grateful to my beloved family and friends for their continuous encouragement, support, and sustenance.

Introduction
Foundations to Build Upon

In this introduction to the book you will find:

1. Fundamental information about assessment literacy.
2. A working vocabulary for assessment.
3. Essential concepts and critical perspectives on assessment.
4. A reflection on using this information to upskill understanding and practice.

Assessment Literacy

Assessment literacy encompasses a broad spectrum of skills and knowledge. In relation to routine practice, assessment-literate teachers understand the role of assessment in a learning culture, can construct dependable assessments, and effectively utilize assessment results. This requires a deep understanding of curriculum and standards, the ability to unpack standards into measurable learning outcomes, purposefully select or design aligned assessment instruments, understand and then utilize the results to responsively inform teaching and learning.

Assessment-literate teachers are skilled in:

1. Designing and selecting assessment instruments.
2. Aligning assessment with the desired standards and learning outcomes.
3. Matching the assessment with the purpose: formative, summative, benchmark.

4. Utilizing multiple methods to assess diverse levels of cognitive complexity.
5. Monitoring student progress towards learning targets.
6. Administering, scoring, and interpreting teacher-produced assessment.
7. Interpreting assessment data in relation to strengths, gaps, growth, and final outcomes.
8. Using assessment results when making decisions about individual students, planning, teaching, developing curriculum, and school improvement.
9. Developing reliable pupil-grading procedures that depend on valid student assessments.
10. Communicating assessment results to students, parents, and other audiences.
11. Recognizing unethical, illegal, and inappropriate assessment methods and uses of assessment information.

Compiled from Sanders (2000) and Kahl, Hofman, and Bryant (2013)

When these ideas are synthesized, a concise definition looks like this: Assessment-literate educators are able to purposefully select, develop and, utilize, throughout teaching and learning, multiple formative, diagnostic, and summative strategies that are aligned with standards-based learning targets and reflect varied levels of cognitive complexity. They effectively collect, monitor, use, and respond to data and evidence that identifies students' strengths, documents growth, and measures outcomes.

Assessment Vocabulary

As you read the chapters, a working vocabulary of assessment is essential. The words test, measure, evaluate, and assess are often intertwined but they are, in fact, each a distinct concept.

TEST is typically an instrument used to measure learning. There are many ways to test from selected choice questions that generally produce one correct answer and result in an objective measure of learning to completion and extended responses such as essays provide insights into students' understanding and analysis and require more complex measures.

MEASURE is a way to assign a number to the test results. If I assign you the number 1 would you know if it was your golf handicap or the balance in your checkbook? 100 could mean the number of correct answers on a test or how much money you lost at bingo. A measure doesn't provide much information unless it has a context.

EVALUATE contains the word value, meaning to give some significance to the measure. When we assign a percentage we recognize that you got 80% of the questions correct or that you read at the 60th percentile. The perspective on the meaning of a number gives it value and relevance.

ASSESS means we use those values to inform our understanding of learning and guide decisions about teaching and learning. Our assessment may be in relation to an individual student, the whole class, grade, or school, and our response may be at each of these levels. Assessment works best when multiple measures are considered.

Quick Quiz on Alignment

Select the two correct responses to the statement. Write the letter of the answer in the space after the statement.

When comparing assessment to measurement _____ and _____

    A. assessment is defined by a single numerical score
    B. assessment provides information that guides instructional decisions
    C. assessment uses multiple measures to provide data
    D. assessment results in a numerical grid showing students' rankings

Self-Assessment: Correct answers are B and C

The Roots of Assessment

An exploration of the source of the word assessment reveals its original intent. It comes from the Latin word *assidere* that combines the words *sedere* meaning "to sit" and *ad* meaning "beside." Over the years, the word assessor has expanded to mean one who fixes the worth of something for taxation and also describes someone who estimates the value of something. In education, assessment has evolved to mean a measure of knowledge and skills and is used to evaluate individuals, classrooms, schools, districts, and the educational system as a whole.

Students have been sitting for tests for centuries, but rarely do teachers sit beside them to coach and guide their work. Perhaps it is time to return to our roots. Rather than using assessment interchangeably with the word measurement (the assignment of a numerical value) we should use it to reflect the teacher and student working together to determine and guide student's growth towards mastery.

Upskilling

It's fun to invent new words—not that I expect to see them in Webster's anytime soon. When I work with students on defining character traits they are more able to understand "stick-to-itiveness" than "perseverance." As one class was discussing the income gap a student proposed the idea of "Nillionaires" as people having little or no money.

In terms of assessment, people are much more receptive to the idea of upskilling what they already know and do. The idea of upskilling means that much of what you will learn in this book you are already doing in some part. It means that you may continue some practices but also look with a critical eye at what you can do to improve or incorporate new strategies. For example, perhaps you have been using a KWL as a pre-assessment but want to develop a deeper understanding of each student's incoming knowledge. You may want to consider using *Plickers* to determine individual levels of knowledge, then follow that up with a collaborative question generation process, and then sort and align the questions with learning targets. Scilla may ask if frogs have stomachs like people do; Rodie wonders why they hop rather than walk on their legs; and Rogera wants to know how to dissect one to see its guts and explains that when he saw one squished on the road, he couldn't tell one organ from another.

Intentional Assessment

"If you don't know where you are going you will probably end up somewhere else" Laurence Peter (1977, p. 125).

How often have you started a unit of instruction with clear learning targets but got distracted by what I like to call "shiny things." This could be a video, guest speaker, current news event, advice from a co-worker, or a new school mandate.

Perhaps you want to learn a new skill such as skiing. On your first try you fall down often and quickly give up. On your second try you find someone who can explain why you are falling down, how to lean differently, or readjust your poles, or offers a more effective way to slow down and stop. With this guidance and support along the way you are able to reach your goal of successfully navigating the beginner slope.

If you travel and arrive at a place where you recall having a wonderful cup of coffee but discover that the coffee shop doesn't seem to be where you remember, what do you do? You've been there before but it looks unfamiliar, so how can you tell you are in the right place? Most of us wouldn't park and wander for hours. Rather we might ask someone, look for familiar landmarks, or check Google maps.

So it is with best practice in assessment. We all need a clear target, with a navigable path, some helpful guidance and support along the path, and regulation of our progress as we move forward. In this way we arrive at the goal in the most beneficial way with evidence of how we did and what we might do differently next time.

Symbiosis

The word symbiosis originates from the Greek words for living and together. It is often used in a scientific context to describe the interaction "between two different organisms living in close physical association typically to the advantage of both" (Oxford Dictionaries, 2016). A symbiotic relationship is beneficial to both sides with each part being dependent on the other. This is similar to the idea of yin and yang when two seemingly diverse forces are interconnected in such a way that each complements the other.

It is this type of reciprocity that must be nurtured in assessment. Rather than an add-on at the conclusion of learning, assessment is an essential and ingrained element of reciprocal teaching and learning. How do we know if students are gaining any traction from the instruction without assessing them? How do we know what to assess if the instructional content and processes aren't evident? Of course you could assess my piano playing by asking me to throw a basketball, but all you would learn is that I was extremely uncoordinated.

The relevance of symbiotic assessment is visible beyond teaching and learning and can be seen in curriculum design, professional development, and reporting. It resonates with a wide range of constituents. It is reflected in a school's learning management system and is mutually beneficial to the entire system of education.

Deconstruction

A seven-year-old asked me "How do you eat an elephant?" When I replied I couldn't do that he said, sure you could, you just have to take it one bite at a time. But the standards elephant as shown in Figure I.1 is large and cumbersome. While symbiosis brings ideas together, the deconstruction of assessment is also an essential part of the spectrum.

Big picture standards describe long-term learning outcomes. These are typically too large, complex, and cumbersome to routinely assess. For example, "recognize patterns in algebraic functions" and "develop claims and counterclaims using evidence" are big picture outcomes of learning.

Figure I.1 The Standards Elephant

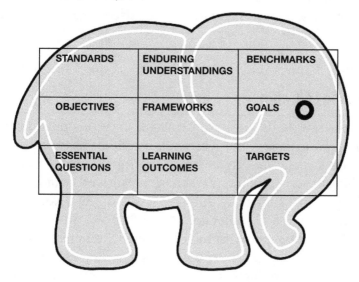

These big picture outcomes must be deconstructed into measurable outcomes that describe the knowledge and skills students are expected to master at the completion of a lesson or unit of instruction. Deconstructed examples include,"apply a substitution strategy for finding the solution to this equation" and "provide at least 2, accurately cited, supporting details for each of your main points." Other terms that will be used interchangeably throughout this book to describe these measurable outcomes include

Table I.1 From Standards to Measurable Learning Targets

Big picture standards	Measurable learning targets
Write routinely for a range of tasks and purposes	Given a sentence written in the past tense, students will be able to rewrite it in the future tense
Reason abstractly and quantitatively	Graph equations with two or more variables on coordinate axes with labels and scales
Sort ideas into two groups by a common attribute	Compare geopolitical, commercial, and cultural characteristics in these three countries

objectives, learning targets, and essential questions. Table I.1 shows how some big picture standards can be deconstructed into measurable outcomes.

Assessing Learning

Once the standards are deconstructed, decisions must be made about how to assess the learning objectives. Some assessment methods such as selected choice (multiple choice, true/false, matching) and completion (fill-in, short answer, data interpretation) are better aligned with lower levels of the taxonomy such as remembering and understanding. When we want students to go higher and deeper with their learning, alternative (sometimes called authentic) assessments are a better choice. Learning outcomes include products, performances, projects, and portfolios. In the book you will find examples of strategies to assess these such as rubrics, checklists, learning contracts/logs, self- and peer assessment. Keep in mind that it is not the strategy you choose, but rather the purposeful alignment with learning outcomes.

Disclaimer: The Challenges of Using Evidence-Based Research

As hard as I have tried to provide support for the ideas in this book, I also recognize that the research that provides many answers also raises many questions. Just when we think we understand the meaning of the marshmallow test, someone refutes it. Mindset, based on years of research at Stanford, also has its detractors. Even in science and medicine, people propose disparate cures for illness. In education it is virtually impossible to control both independent and dependent variables while doing no harm to students who may miss out on learning opportunities or be subjected knowingly to ineffective practice.

We can give the same test to groups of students but we can't control their diet, sleep patterns, or socioeconomic and cultural influences. This is also the case with much psychological and sociological research. Even in the sciences, the control groups may have significant differences in compliance and inaccuracies in reporting effects. Educational research has gotten better and will continue to improve but schools will continue to be a complex mixture of communities, cultures, teachers, students, facilities, resources, and more. As you read this book, consider and select the best evidence-based practices to upskill your local assessment practices and improve learning outcomes for your students.

Reflection on Assessment Literacy

Individual:

1. On a 1 to 10 scale use a blue marker to indicate your current understanding of assessment literacy and a green marker for where you would like to be.

   Analysis of my current understanding and skills in assessment:

This is all new to me							Highly skilled		
1	2	3	4	5	6	7	8	9	10

2. What assessment practices do I presently use and in what ways? How would I like to upskill them?

For a discussion group:

1. What steps can we take to develop and strengthen the symbiotic relationship between learning and assessing?

2. How can we deconstruct complex standards into teachable and assessable portions of learning?

1

Purposeful Assessment

Objectives of this chapter

1. Construct purposeful and planned assessments.
2. Apply strategies for building aligned and progressive assessments.
3. Utilize sequenced and cyclical models of assessment.
4. Realize the value of reciprocal and responsive assessment.

Planned, Progressive, and Cyclical

Assessment has many purposes that range from minute by minute check-ins for understanding to high-stakes and large-scale tests. Warwick Mansell and Mary James (2009) explain that "the nature and impact of assessment depends on the uses to which the results of that assessment are put" (p. 5). Generating internal information that is instructionally useful for students and teachers is different from using high-stakes testing to judge a school, state, or country. Rarely can one type of assessment be suitable to this wide range of contexts.

I have a friend who is a professional planner and organizer. She started her business after 25 years as a classroom teacher and relies on those experiences to successfully build her practice. What people like is her ability to sort through the clutter and organize their materials and practices to facilitate the best long-term improvement.

Many of those same skills and outcomes are part of purposeful assessment at the local level. First is knowing where you and your students are now and where they are headed. Once you have determined this starting point and direction, you need a plan for getting there. It's great to say I want all my students to focus on accuracy in writing informative texts that examine topics and convey ideas. But this requires sorting through the clutter and deconstructing the writing process to align with targeted planning and assessments in order to close gaps in knowledge and skills. It may be that Gregor is highly skilled in writing opening sentences and paragraph construction but doesn't understand the difference between informative and persuasive writing. Perhaps Magrite needs guidance in finding accurate information or assistance in precisely sequencing steps.

It is only when we ask about what is important to measure, what are the consequences of the measure, and how will the data be used, that we can be purposeful in our selection, implementation, and analysis of assessment.

Planning for Assessment

Teaching is a constant cycle of planning, instructing, assessing, and responding. This cycle takes place throughout all the layers of the educational system. Nationally, there are comprehensive standards that are measured with large-scale tests. Then, there are state and content area curricula. Locally, there are regional and school-based instructional maps, sequences, and plans. All of these, each in their own way, inform teachers in the preparation, delivery, and assessment of daily lessons.

At the same time, not all of the large-scale standards are assessed on national and state tests. For example, there are no questions asking a student to "analyze various accounts of a subject told in different mediums." So how does a teacher go about measuring student achievement on these overlooked standards?

Local curriculum may include recommended assessments such as a common grade level test, or a rubric for a poster on alternative energy sources. But, in general, the scoring criteria are left to the teacher's discretion. Units of instruction typically suggest assessment strategies. This may include a weekly quiz or an ongoing log of learning outcomes, but leave the actual evaluation of the student's achievement to the classroom teacher.

There are literally thousands of standards, some measured by standardized tests but others within the jurisdiction of the classroom teacher. When hundreds of standards, with only some measured by traditional measures, are combined with nominal guidance on planning classroom assessment, it becomes the teacher's responsibility for knowing what students know, understand, and can do.

The Eberly Center for Teaching Excellence and Educational Innovation at Carnegie Mellon explains that "Alignment increases the probability that we will provide students with the opportunities to learn, and practice the skills and knowledge required on the assessments. Alignment means that good grades translate into good learning." Planning for assessment is just as, if not more important, as planning for teaching and learning. Both need to be done with purpose and precision.

Teaching as a Continual Act of Assessment

Planning a unit of instruction typically begins with the standards that the students are aiming towards. An important consideration in this is how well students have mastered previously learned standards and also where are they expected to be at the end of teaching and learning.

If you had minimal experience making pizza and you wanted to make a tasty one for a child's birthday party you might search for different recipes, ask friends for theirs, or watch a chef on the Food Network. Each of these sources may suggest a different type of leavening (fast vs. slow acting yeast), varied sauces from bottled ones to home-made versions, as well as selection of cheeses and toppings. You comply with the expert's guidance as best you can but the pizza is mediocre. How can you tell why it didn't turn out better? Was it the way you kneaded the dough, the time to let it rise, or the quality of the sauce? Each of these questions requires thoughtful analysis.

Teachers use a variety of instructional strategies from teacher-guided instruction, to student-directed learning, to a gradual release of responsibility to the student. Teachers must also use a variety of assessment strategies to determine how well students mastered the targets. As with the pizza, this requires multiple types of assessment throughout teaching and learning in order to produce the optimum results.

Deliberate Assessment

Teaching and assessing is also a continuous process of problem solving and adjusting practice. From large-scale standards through checking on progress minute by minute, teachers need a toolbox of well-honed yet malleable strategies. The selection and fine-tuning of the strategies requires knowledge of students' strengths as well as areas for growth. It also requires that a teacher be purposeful in their selection, be focused in their use, be precise in timing, and accurate in their interpretation. This means understanding why, when, what, and how to continuously monitor learning.

Seven Questions to Guide Deliberate Assessment Practice:

1. What are the most important standards and learning targets (a.k.a., goals and objectives)?
2. What are my students' current knowledge and skills?
3. What are the desired student learning outcomes? Is this the same for all learners?
4. How will I assess progress towards goals?
5. How will I measure learning outcomes?
6. How will I respond to this information?
7. What modifications will I make along the way?

The Value of Blueprints

After building several homes I realized that without detailed blueprints the results might not be as expected. In one house where I wanted an open floor plan, it didn't occur to me that the living, dining, and kitchen areas had no visible partitions. This was great in theory, but in practice made for a noisy, visually complex area, not the calming open space I imagined. After that, I learned to study the blueprints more carefully to not only see the floor level, but also to envision the 3-D perspective. Fortunately a few half walls and columns solved the problem.

An assessment blueprint can serve some of these same purposes. It provides the groundwork by providing a floor level view of assessment while guiding the alignment of learning outcomes with assessment strategies. Basically a blueprint identifies the learning goals, the depth of learning, and the strategies for assessing. It insures that the assessments are interconnected and purposeful. Figure 1.1 shows how this works to make certain that all elements of the assessment are in harmony with their purpose.

Figure 1.1 Basics of Alignment

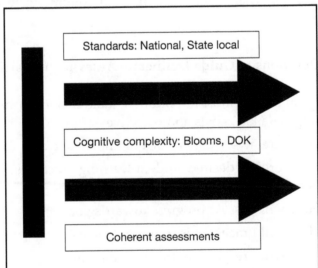

Standards: National, State local

Cognitive complexity: Blooms, DOK

Coherent assessments

It makes little sense to give a multiple choice test on students analysis and evaluation of primary source material. Nor is it reasonable to measure a big picture standard such as "Develop understanding of fractions as numbers" with an essay. Accurate alignment is an important early step in planning for assessment.

One of the most effective strategies for deliberately planning and assessing is through the use of a blueprint. There are many versions of this. Sometimes it is called a table of specifications. Regardless of the model you choose, a blueprint delineates the standards, content, types, and levels of assessment. It guides instructional processes and ensures alignment with learning outcomes and their assessment. A blank blueprint is shown in Table 1.1.

As a teacher starts to populate the blueprint, it begins to show the learning targets, the types of assessment strategies, and the levels of complexity. If desired the blueprint can also include point values and weighting of various assessments. Table 1.2 shows how the test blueprint looks in progress.

Now that you've seen the basic construction of a blueprint, Table 1.3 shows one created by a student teacher. When he arrived in this classroom there was a wealth of instructional resources, along with a large amount of teacher-presented information but to his dismay only selected choice tests. When he explained the value of alternative types of assessment and the construction of a blueprint, his mentor teacher encouraged him to prepare one for this instructional unit. Note how he customized the blueprint by identifying two categories of multiple questions and combined fill-in with constructed response.

Below are a few examples of the test questions (see p. 19). They are numbered to match each learning outcome. Directions are included in the original test document.

Table 1.1 Test Blueprint Format

List the Learning Outcomes in Taxonomy Sequence Incorporate Standards from CCSS, Curriculum . . .	Multiple Choice	T/F	Matching	Fill-in/Completion	Constructed Response	Extended Response	Authentic/Alternative	Total	Remember	Understand	Apply	Analyze	Evaluate	Create	Total
Students will define . . . (Remember)															
Students will recognize . . . (Understand)															
Students will use . . . (Apply)															
Students will collaboratively compare . . . (Analyze)															
Students will critique . . . (Evaluate)															
Students will produce . . . (Create)															
Total # of Questions															

Table 1.2 Test Blueprint in Progress

List the Learning Outcomes in Taxonomy Sequence Incorporate Standards from CCSS, Curriculum . . . Show the number of questions by level	Multiple Choice	T/F	Matching	Fill-in/Completion	Constructed Response	Extended Response	Authentic/Alternative	Total	Remember	Understand	Apply	Analyze	Evaluate	Create	Total
Students will define personal narrative using topical vocabulary	3	3						6	6						6
Students will recognize narrative techniques (dialogue, pacing, description, tone) in classroom examples		3		3				6		6					6
Students will use narrative techniques in their own personal narrrative					1			1			1				1
Students will engage in whole class discussion comparing personal narrative to other types of writing						1	1	2				2			2
Students will evaluate the effectiveness of different personal narrative techniques by . . .					3			3					3		3
Students will use technology to produce an illustrated personal narrative							1	1						1	1
Total # of Questions								19							19

Table 1.3 Populated Blueprint

List the Learning Outcomes in Taxonomy Sequence Incorporate Standards from CCSS, Curriculum ...	MC-fact.	MC-comp.	T/F	Matching	Short Answer	Extended	Authentic/Alternative	Total	Remember	Understand	Apply	Analyze	Evaluate	Create	Total
1. Recall events and commanders at the Battle of Gettysburg. **Remember**			2		2			4	4						4
2. Describe the sequence of events at the Battle of Gettysburg. **Remember**	2	1	1					4	4						4
3. Recognize the procedures and tactics of soldiers during the Civil War. **Understand**	1				2			3		3					3
4. Explain the challenges of commanding troops during the Civil War. **Understand**					1			1		1					1
5. Examine maps to understand how geography and topography affected the battle. **Apply**						1		1			1				1
6. Justify and critique the decisions made by the commanders at Gettysburg. **Evaluate**						1		1					1		1
7. Reconstruct what commanders should have done differently to cause alternate war outcomes. Write a story from one person/s perspective. **Create**							1	1						1	1
Total # of Questions	3	1	3		5	2	1	15	8	4	1		1	1	15

Examples of Test Questions

1) _____ T/F General Pickett protested General Lee's decision to attack the Union center at Cemetery Ridge. *(Remember)*

3) One major strategy of units during the Civil War was to get around the enemies' sides, also known as their _____. *(Understand)*

5) Using the map (on p. 20), write an essay explaining which army had the more favorable position during the Battle of Gettysburg? Use names of specific places and features on your map to support your reasoning. Then, explain to what degree the geography of the battlefield influenced the outcome of the battle? Integrate visual information (e.g., in charts, graphs, photographs, videos, or maps) with other information in print and digital texts). *(Apply)*

6) Based on their effect on the Battle of Gettysburg, rank the following Union Officers in order of importance (1=most important). Place the rank (1–4) before each name. After each name, give at least one specific action or decision that he made that influenced your decision. *(Evaluate)*

___ General Hancock _____
___ Colonel Chamberlain _____
___ General Meade _____
___ General Pickett _____

7) In his memoirs (autobiography), written years later, General Longstreet recorded what he said to Lee before Pickett's Charge:

> "I have been a soldier, I may say, from the ranks up to the position I now hold. I have been in pretty much all kinds of skirmishes, from those of two or three soldiers up to those of an army corps, and I think I can safely say there never was a body of fifteen thousand men who could make that attack successfully."

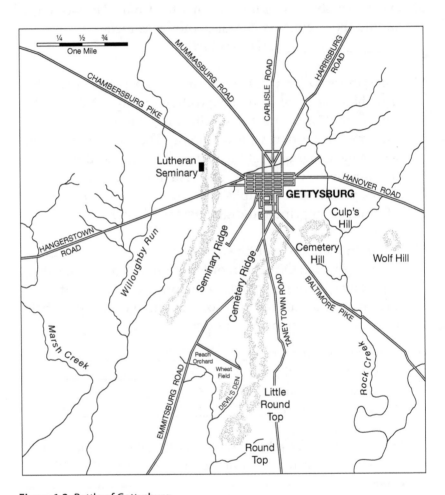

Figure 1.2 Battle of Gettysburg

Do you think that General Longstreet is correct in his reasoning? Why or why not. Using what you know about the Battle of Gettysburg as well as Civil War tactics, give three specific reasons for your argument.

(Distinguish among fact, opinion, and reasoned judgment in a text.) *(Create)*

Reflection on Planning Assessment Using Blueprints

Step 1

1. What areas of alignment did you recognize in this student's example?
2. What suggestion would you give to the student to strengthen his alignment?

Step 2

How will you use these ideas to inform and upskill your own planning?

Deconstructing Standards

At the heart of planning for assessment is the essential step of deconstructing standards. Big picture standards are typically too complex to measure but within the big standards are measurable nuggets of learning. For example, an eighth grade standard for reading informational texts says "Read closely to determine what the text says explicitly and to make logical inferences from it; cite specific textual evidence when writing or speaking to support conclusions drawn from the text."

Within this are several learning outcomes:

◆ What is the difference between explicit and inferred meaning of a text?
◆ What does it mean (look like in practice) to cite evidence in support of conclusions?
◆ How can you use highlighting, notes, and graphic organizers to sort through the information and identify the author's main ideas?

◆ What strategies does the author use to emphasize and reinforce his main ideas?

The next step is to deconstruct the standards into measurable chunks of learning as shown in Table 1.4.

Table 1.4 Deconstructing Standards

Standard	Assessable learning target
Example: Use multiplication and division within 100 to solve word problems in situations involving equal groups, arrays, and measurement quantities, e.g., by using drawings and equations with a symbol for the unknown number to represent the problem.	Create visual representations of one-step math problems. Produce an array model of multiplication. Use drawings of equal groups to solve a problem.
Example: Analyze how complex characters (those with multiple or conflicting motivations) develop over the course of a text, interact with other characters, and advance the plot or develop the theme.	Define multiple traits of the two main characters in the story. Use our character chart to describe how the motives represented multiple diverse or conflicting traits. How would the plot change if one of the characters were to change their beliefs or behaviors? Write a different ending to the story.
Select one of your big picture standards and deconstruct it into measurable learning targets.	

Taking this idea to the next level, Table 1.5 shows the standard, assessable learning targets, and suggested assessment strategies.

Table 1.5 Deconstructed Standards with Assessments

Content standard, or local goal/ target	Instructional objectives/learning target and instructional strategies	Describe the type of assessment i.e., selected choice, completion, essay, alternative (type). Identify the level of the taxonomy
Speaking and Listening, K-12 Participate effectively in a range of conversations and collaborations with diverse partners, building on each other's ideas and expressing their own ideas clearly and persuasively.	Define terms related to recycling: reduce, reuse, repurpose, etc. Describe ways to recycle at home and school. Working with a small team, students will create persuasive brochures explaining strategies and benefits of recycling at home.	Student-generated quiz questions on vocabulary and key ideas of recycling: these are compiled by the teacher into a quiz. *(Remembering and Understanding)* A rubric with a 4 point range of achievement levels (exemplary, proficient, basic, novice) on: – contribution to the group – active and respectful listening/responding – accuracy of content – use of facts to persuade – applied technology – self-assessment and peer review of research strategies, synthesis of ideas, urge to action. *(Application and Creating)*
Use ratio and rate reasoning to solve real-world and mathematical problems, e.g., by reasoning about tables or equivalents, tape diagrams, double number line diagrams, and equations. Find a percent of a quantity as a rate per 100 (e.g., 30% of a quantity means 30/100 times the quantity); solve problems involving finding the whole given a part and the percent.	Understand that a percent is the rate per 100. Understand that percentage-based rate problems compare two different units where one of the units is 100. Recognize that these can be represented using tape diagrams, line diagrams, and equations. Write percent as a rate over 100. Given parts and a percent, determine the whole.	**A world of ratios:** Post a graffiti wall with students' examples of how ratio, rate, and percent are used in their world. *(Application)* **Students write word problems** after teacher-directed instruction. Along with a problem of the day for each day of the unit. *(Understanding)* **Class challenge:** With another class hold a math decathlon using student-generated questions (checked by the teacher). *(4Cs: Critical Thinking, Communication, Collaboration, Creativity)* **Application cards:** Describe ways their new knowledge can be used in the real world. Explain how they would use rates, fractions, and percents and how they can be solved with diagrams. Write 2 real-world problems Solve 4 real-world problems
Your application:		

Checkpoint on Deconstructing Standards

How will you apply these ideas to modify and upskill your practice?

1. Select one big picture standard then deconstruct it into teachable chunks.
2. Clearly describe the measurable learning targets and indicators of success.
3. Purposefully select instructional strategies to support student achievement.
4. Select and/or design multiple measures that align with the learning outcomes.

Summary of steps in planning for assessment:

1. Start with the Big Picture
   A. Maintain a focus on the standards and learning outcomes.
   B. Start with big picture standards that you can deconstruct into teachable chunks.

2. Translate to Local Practice
   A. Establish daily learning outcomes that are specific and measurable for learners.
   B. Identify criteria for success and strategies for supporting student achievement.

3. Align Instruction
   A. Verify that instructional strategies support the learning outcomes.
   B. Engage students as learners and assessors.

4. Plan Assessment Purposefully
   A. Select and/or design assessments that align with the learning outcomes.
   B. Use multiple measures and differentiation to support the diversity of learners.

5. Respond
   A. Collect, verify, and analyze demonstrations of learning.
   B. Respond to the students' evidence of learning.

In Practice: Putting Assessment First

In science class, Jamal finds the topics fascinating but challenging and quickly turns off when the information becomes too complex. He puts his head down and tells Ms. Sindor that he is too tired to learn. She has seen this ploy before. After several years of practice she can tell the tricksters from the true sleepy-heads. She too, has some tricks up her sleeve. She recognizes that she has little control over how her students arrive at school, but she knows that she has total control over her response to them.

In a traditional classroom the teacher typically plans the unit and then at the end decides how to test the students. In order to gain the most traction on the path to learning, the distance and finishing line must be clear from the start. After all, who would run a marathon with no ending point or worse, a constantly changing one? Backwards design is universal in the business world and useful in education. Stephen Covey (1998) explained this concept in *7 Habits of Highly Effective Teens*. The definitive work on this topic in education is *Understanding by Design* from Grant Wiggins and Jay McTighe (2005). Yet these aren't new ideas, as Søren Kierkegaard in 1843 philosophized: "Life can only be understood backwards, but it must be lived forwards."

A reversal in planning means starting with the outcomes in mind. In this way, students know where they are heading and, with guidance, can choose the best path to take them there. They also know the markers along the way and what they will find at the end of the trek. Will it be a desk with a bubble sheet, a tablet with an essay question, a real problem to solve, or a wise sage asking more questions?

Ms. Sindor starts planning her middle school science unit with the outcomes in mind. The learning targets are:

1. Define the structure and function of parts of the digestive system. *(Science Curriculum)*
2. Demonstrate the physical and chemical processes of digestion. *(Science Curriculum)*
3. Determine the meaning of key terms . . . as they are used in a specific scientific context.
4. Follow precisely, a multistep procedure when carrying out experiments . . . or performing technical tasks.
5. Design and construct a model of the human digestive system to accomplish its functions of breakdown, absorption, and elimination. *(Taxonomy: Creating)*

In order to assess her students' incoming knowledge she begins by having them label and describe parts of the digestive system. Then, like an architect, uses that as a foundation to fine-tune the unit and its assessments. She predetermines the evidence of learning and the level that students must achieve to be deemed proficient. She asks herself what is most important for students to know and be able to do with their learning, and what kind of assessment will provide that evidence. She considers strategies to engage the students in assessment and how to design it to reveal their best work. Her unit includes traditional measures of content knowledge as well as constructed responses to show understanding, along with authentic performance tasks where students can demonstrate their ability to apply learning and innovating. Assessments are strategically placed before, during, and after learning.

Please keep in mind the ideas throughout this book are intended to be descriptive rather than prescriptive. Telling teachers how to assess doesn't work as each student, teacher, classroom, school, and district and state are unique. At the same time there are common foundations for quality assessment that will continue to be emphasized throughout the book.

Aligned and Progressive Assessments

In the last section we talked about the importance of making purposeful decisions when planning for assessment. Moving forward with those ideas, in this section we will focus on the value of assessment that is aligned and also the steps to take to make sure that happens. Paul La Marca (2001) explains that "Alignment refers to the degree of match between test content and the subject area content identified through state and national academic standards" (p. 1). He goes on to describe two overarching dimensions: Content match means alignment with the standards from large-scale to classroom. Depth match refers to the level of learning complexity that the assessment is measuring.

If we want to know how well students have learned what was intended for them to learn, then assessment must accurately reflect the learning targets as well as instruction. I recently listened to a student complain that she had studied really hard for her history test. She reviewed notes and classroom handouts only to discover that the unit test was based solely on the textbook that the teacher never mentioned in class. When I listened to her concerns and took a look at her notebook, it was difficult to find a mention of the learning targets amid all the events and historical figures.

This same student told me how poorly she performed on multiple choice tests. Always narrowing it down to two possible answers, she invariably chose the wrong one. This is an important reminder that along with powerful alignment with the learning targets, additional multiple methods are vital for assessing different types of learning at different levels and depths.

To reiterate, assessment is most powerful when it is fully aligned with planning, teaching, and learning. Throughout this process it is essential for students to have opportunities to practice, apply, and develop mastery of specific learning targets. Only when this happens do the results from the assessments accurately reflect student achievement.

Alignment with Learning Targets

Content matching requires alignment throughout the spectrum of standards from broad scale to subject area, and classroom learning targets. The essential question is: How accurately do the assessments uncover and display student progress toward targets throughout the lesson, unit, or year?

Depth matching refers to the level of complexity that the assessment requires. This can range from recall of knowledge to demonstration of a new skill or creation of an original product. For example, assessing a student's ability to sequence the stages of photosynthesis requires a lower cognitive level in the assessment. Asking a student to design an experiment to determine how carbon dioxide in the earth's troposphere affects photosynthesis requires a more complex assessment of deeper understanding. Here are a few more examples:

Recall: Student defines, restates, describes
          Assessed with selected choice, completion,
          highlighting, labeling

Apply: Student organizes, compares, modifies,
          estimates, observes
          Assessed with concept map, accuracy of blog
          entry calculation

Evaluate: Student critiques, investigates, solves, concludes
          Assessed with rubrics and learning logs for
          debate, database, storyboard, Socratic seminar

Create: Student designs, synthesizes, produces
          Assessed with rubrics and self/peer review of
          website, research, documentary

Questions to consider about alignment:

1. Are the assessments aligned with the instructional purpose?
2. What evidence is being gathered?
3. What inferences are being made about teachers and learners?
4. How is this used to make informed decisions about curriculum, instructional practices, resources, and teacher development?

With the depth and complexity of large-scale standards, it is unlikely one test can show all of what a student knows and can do. Drilling down through all layers of assessment regulations, systems, classrooms, teachers, and learners is essential to ensure alignment. Doing so also minimizes the focus on final scores while emphasizing the significance of using assessment results to make decisions about systems as well as individual learners.

Alignment Through Progressions

According to the Glossary of Education Reform (2013), learning progressions refer to the "Purposeful sequencing of teaching and learning expectations . . . that map out a specific sequence of knowledge and skills that students are expected to learn as they progress through their education." Karin Hess (2008) at the National Center for Improvement in Education Assessment adds to that with her Guiding Principle II "Learning progressions have clear binding threads that articulate the essential/core concepts and processes" (p. 4). Progressions are the basic building blocks of learning that guide students towards mastery. Progressions also support and validate the alignment of standards and assessment in all subjects from math and spelling, to digital literacy and atomic theory. The large-scale standards are written as progressing, but in general, are not granular enough to guide daily classroom assessment. Here are two brief examples of increasingly complex learning progressions context areas.

A progression for reading:

1. Recognize letters.
2. Produce a sound for each letter.
3. Construct knowledge of graphemes and phonemes.
4. Sound out increasingly complex words.
5. Use a variety of decoding strategies.
6. Decode age-appropriate texts fluently.

In science a progression of earth/space science looks like this:

K–2: There are patterns of movement to the sun, moon, and stars

Table 1.6 Progressions Through the Taxonomy

Planning: Learning targets	Teaching: Instructional strategy and aligned technology	Learning: Engaging students	Assessment: Multiple and aligned
Remembering Make sense of core content	Describe characteristics of the seasons: using models, viewings, readings. *Quizlet*	Growing plants and melting ice. Draw/Illustrate seasons. Physically move around the sun.	Label a diagram of seasons. Tell it to a Martian (explain in your own words). Assess vocabulary for accuracy.
Understanding Explain and organize content	Participate in Literature Circles to compare genres based on style, content, and form. *Storybird*	Individual book reviews; whole class sorting of types of literature.	Design concept maps: explain genres, provide examples. Assess accuracy and explanations.
Apply Use, sort, and demonstrate learning	Students classify their walk-about observations into animal, vegetable, or mineral. *Coggle.it*	Students use mind maps to display learning.	Self-assessment comparing the classes; sorting categories.
Evaluating Draw conclusions about core content	Display and analyze real-world math (as appropriate to grade level) using global statistics. *Google Hangouts*	Students use global data to write their own math problems. They write questions and sponsor a Math Challenge.	Assess students' questions for accuracy and real-world connections. Measure accuracy of process and answers during Math Challenge.
Creating Produce original works about core content	Invent a new insect based on what you know about their characteristics and life cycle. *SumoPaint*	Based on our understanding of the purpose of parts of insects, design insects of the future.	Create an original and scientifically sound model of an insect and its life cycle. Assess accuracy, originality, support for design.

3–5: The earth's orbit and rotation can be observed.

6–8: The solar system contains objects held together by gravity.

9–12: Kepler's laws explain the motion of orbiting objects.

These progressions then inform teaching, learning, and assessing. Table 1.6, based on Bloom's revised Taxonomy (Anderson and Krathwohl, 2001), offers a brief example of teaching and assessing at different levels of learning.

Assessment that Supports Learning

Here is an example of a deconstructed large-scale standard in Mr. Roberts' classroom:

Calculate the correct measure (perimeter, area, or volume), by identifying key words and ideas in a word problem.

✓ Lesson Objectives: Design a park: determine which measures to use for sandbox, water rapids with a round pool, ball field, playhouse, and gardens.

✓ Instructional Design: Students construct a computer model or a 3-D design of a new park.

✓ Student Engagement: Embellish your park and calculate the space needed for components such as fences, trees, and other play areas.

✓ Assessment: Checklists, rubrics, and answer keys for use of correct measures, mathematical accuracy. Collaboration and presentation skills may also be included. Summative individual tests on applied measurement using calculations and real-world scenarios for problem solving.

From a student view this lesson has many sticky elements (see Chapter 3). It is of interest to children, there are opportunities for choice, it makes real-world connections to the standards, and assessment is embedded right into teaching and learning. It can become even more a real-world scenario if the local PTA or community is actually planning to build a new playground.

Table 1.7 provides question prompts at each level of Bloom's Taxonomy. Keep in mind that this is not an exact science as a prompt using the word "describe" could be at the understanding level as in "Explain the meaning of these poetic contractions: 'tis, o'er, ne'er." Alternatively students could be asked to explain why they believe the school day should begin at a later hour. In their

Table 1.7 Question Prompts Through the Taxonomy

Level	Descriptors	Prompts/Questions
Remember	Define, Identify, Label, List, Name, Recall, State	Where is, Who was, Which one, When did, How many, Name the, Label the, Name three, Find the shape, Write the formula for
Understand	Describe, Explain, Recognize, Restate, Select, Summarize	In your own words, Give an example of, Describe what or how, Clarify the main idea, Is this the same as, What does the image/table mean, What does it represent
Apply	Demonstrate, Illustrate, Implement, Solve, Utilize, Show how	What if you, What would you do differently, How would you use, How would you resolve, What are the results of, Is there another situation that, Draw a diagram that, Demonstrate a way to, Solve for
Analyze	Attribute, Categorize, Compare, Differentiate, Distinguish, Examine, Integrate, Organize, Sort	What other ways are there to, What would happen if, How are they alike/different, What caused, Why did he, Which are facts/opinions, What is the purpose of, What's their point of view, What is the relationship between, What were the motives behind
Evaluate	Appraise, Argue, Assess, Critique, Debate, Defend, Judge, Justify, Rank, Rate, Support	What's a better way to, Which is most important, Was it good or bad, How would you defend that idea, What would you change, What's your conclusion, What fallacies do you see, Find the errors, What are the consequences of, Weigh the pros and cons
Create	Assemble, Compile, Construct, Design, Devise, Formulate, Generate, Invent, Produce, Synthesize	Pretend you are, Design a, Build a, Write a different ending, What would have happened if, What would you add to it, If you had the resources how or what would you make or improve

responses they may apply the research they read or use their knowledge of time zones to compare the pros and cons, and propose an original solution within their explanations.

Quick Quiz on Alignment

Compare the alignment in these two questions. Which one is better aligned with the level of Bloom's taxonomy?

Question 1

Learning Target: Use sentence-level context to *interpret* the meaning of a word or phrase.

Assessment: *Define* these terms

Abolish _____

Protagonist _____

Tropical _____

Question 2

Learning Target: Identify American migration patterns in the 1800s. (CCSS RH.2)

Assessment: *Explain* how this map and its map features show westward expansion in the 1800s.

Analysis: By looking at the verbs in the learning target there is better alignment in question 2 between identify and explain than in question one where the target is to interpret but the question asks to simply define.

In Practice: Insights into Alignment

In one school, the teachers noticed that fraction-based word problems were a problem for many students. The problems typically read something like this: Workmen use half of a pallet of pavers to build 3 steps into the school. Each step was the same size. How many pallets or parts of pallets did they use for each step? Many students were getting it wrong.

If we make the inference that teachers aren't spending enough time teaching and students aren't putting enough effort into practicing, there is a possibility of being incorrect unless we delve into the alignment of standard and instructional strategy. What became visible was that the students could solve the problem using manipulatives and graphic images, but when the problems were presented only numerically, they were unable to simply flip one of the fractions over. The teachers recognized that it wasn't the idea of flipping the fraction, but rather the word problem itself that was creating an alignment problem. They decided to teach a rap song: keep, change, flip (available on YouTube) to help the students learn the formula and immediately saw improvement. They also retaught students how to deconstruct word problems.

When assessments are symbiotic, they are fully aligned from start to finish. In the classroom a teacher can identify the student's current knowledge and skills and make visible any gaps between that and the learning outcomes. This is the place where the process, content, and resources are adjusted and additional supports are put into place. On the large-scale level, intermittent data can guide changes to curriculum, instructional resources, and professional development. Use the concept map in Table 1.8 to create your own aligned sequence of teaching, learning, and assessing.

Table 1.8 Alignment Concept Map

Planning: Learning targets that link to clearly articulated standards	Teaching: Instructional strategies that support standards and curricular targets	Learning: Engaging students as active learners and owners of their learning	Assessing: Multiple strategies that reflect and support the learning outcomes

Sequenced and Cyclical Assessment

The larger and farther away the standards are from a student's day to day learning, the less meaning they have to them. For

example, it means little to the student to: "Use combined knowledge of all letter-sound correspondences, syllabication patterns,
and morphology (e.g., roots and affixes) to read accurately
unfamiliar multisyllabic words in context and out of context."

The closer to the action the standards are, the more likely
the student will be engaged in learning and prepared for the
assessment. Deconstructing the big standards results in local
practice that supports explicit outcomes. This is where students
and teachers are most accountable. It is at this level where learning
outcomes are most assessable. "While learning outcomes are meant
to have a clear relationship to assessment, in practice this tends to
be a somewhat confused area. . . . All learning outcomes should
be written in terms that enable assessment of student learning"
(Moon, 2005, p. 16).

Beyond the idea of deconstructed learning progressions is the
bigger picture concept of sequences and cycles of assessment.

From Large-Scale To Classroom

In the order of learning targets, large-scale standards are the
farthest away from the learner and embedded formative assessments are closest to the learner as shown in Figure 1.3.

Figure 1.3 Progression of Assessment Targets

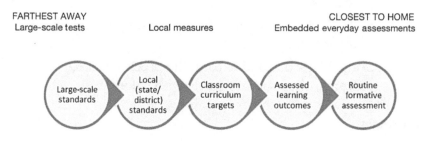

Consider the challenge or ease of preparing assessments for these
two sets of standards.

Set 1: Large-Scale Standards

1. *ELA*: Use knowledge of language and its conventions
   when writing, speaking, reading, or listening.

2. *ELA*: Determine the meaning of figurative and connotative language and analyze the impacts of specific word choices on meaning and tone including analogies or allusions to other texts.

3. *Social Studies*: Integrate quantitative or technical analysis with qualitative analysis in print or digital text.

4. *Math*: Write simple expressions that record calculations with numbers, and interpret numerical expressions without evaluating them.

5. *Science*: Construct and revise an explanation for the outcome of a simple chemical reaction based on the outermost electron state of atoms, trends in the periodic table, and knowledge of the patterns of chemical properties.

Set 2: Local Standards

1. *ELA*: Analyze the author's use of figurative language to express a character's thoughts and feelings. Include specific examples.

2. *Math*: Evaluate numerical expressions containing parentheses.

3. *Social Studies*: Recognize the role of scarcity and how it impacts people's lives.

4. *Science*: Describe and explain the process and outcome when sodium reacts with chlorine.

Classroom

In the classroom, the local standards are translated into units of instruction and lesson plans. Units can range from three or four days up to three to four weeks depending on the complexity of the objective, instructional strategies, and assessment methods. Teachers then design daily lessons that incorporate a variety of assessments from interim benchmark tests, to traditional strategies, alternative methods, and embedded formative assessments.

Checkpoint on Alignment

The second standard on the above list of large-scale standards could be written about the Emma Lazarus poem, "The New Colossus," that says "Give me your tired, your poor, your huddled masses yearning to be free." Yet, on a typical common core test, students are asked:

In that sentence, the word yearning most clearly means:

A. pushing
B. searching
C. desiring
D. afraid.

In this example, C is the best answer but doesn't provide accurate insight into a student's ability to analyze the impact of specific words on meaning and tone.

A teacher seeking to improve this question in her classroom may have the students read a page or two of a text and then ask them to rewrite the immigrant experience through the eyes of the people coming to America for the first time using at least three of these words in their chronicle: Exile, immigrant, tempest, wretched, teeming.

Taking this idea one step further, students can read about more recent immigrant incidents and compare them to "The New Colossus" in relation to the language used and how the experiences are alike and different.

This concept will be revisited throughout the book as you consider assessment in relation to standards and learning targets. When this all aligns with informative assessment, it helps learning stick.

Recurring Cycles

The sequence of targets from broadest to narrowest and farthest to nearest informs an ongoing cycle of assessment designed to improve learning outcomes. Figure 1.4 introduces a cycle that is coherent in its sequence yet flexible in its application. This cycle incorporates the assessment sequence in a way that strongly supports local practice. Note that you can find many versions of this cycle online. In Margaret Heritage's model, the emphasis is on formative assessment. The University of Connecticut puts school mission in the center of the cycle. In one district, they chose to put the students at the center of the cycle. There's more than one right way as long as the emphasis is on purposeful alignment, students' learning, ongoing monitoring, and responsive teaching.

Figure 1.4 The Cycle of Assessment

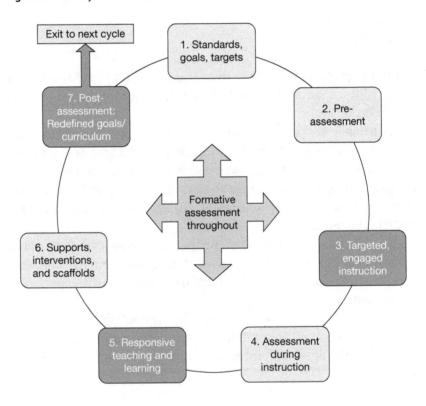

As information about learning is gathered, analyzed, and acted on, data informs each step. This includes an understanding of the current status, the desired outcomes, and actions needed in order to effectively complete the teaching/learning/assessment loop.

Below is a brief description of each step in the cycle:

1. Planning based on alignment with standards, goals, and learning targets identified in curriculum and other guiding documents.
2. Incoming knowledge, understanding, and skills are assessed using multiple methods.
3. Delivery of targeted, aligned, and engaging instruction.
4. Interim monitoring, routine formative assessments, analysis of ongoing learning, interpretation of evidence of learning.
5. Recalibration of teaching and learning to address weak spots; close gaps by adjusting pacing, content, depth, resources, etc.
6. Identify and provide additional supports, scaffolds, and instructional modifications on an as-needed basis.
7. Utilize assessment to inform changes to curriculum, learning targets, and methodology.

Using the Assessment Cycle

◆ Consider your school's and district's instructional policies, regulations, and curriculum mandates.
◆ Translate large-scale standards into local measurable goals and targets.
◆ Plan for purposeful and aligned instructional sequences.
◆ Select formative assessments to elicit specific evidence and monitor ongoing progress.
◆ Respond and recalibrate: Provide feedback, adjust instruction, scaffold/enrich learning.

Lisbeth Gyllander (2013) describes some challenges in developing this type of internally monitored assessment practice rather than an externally imposed system. At the macro level educational directives, administrative factors, curriculum design, and professional development can support or constrain this process. At the micro level teachers' ability to clarify targets, engage students, develop individual plans, and provide feedback will insure or challenge successful implementation.

In Practice

After working with several schools on the design and application of assessment cycles I've learned that there is no one right or best way to implement them. One school wanted to support teachers as they planned and delivered classroom assessments. To do so they provided insights into each step at brief weekly sessions. Some sessions were delivered before or after school and others were available online. For teachers who wanted more information on a topic, in-depth monthly sessions were offered.

The most popular of these were on pre-assessment where teachers learned how to construct questions that would provide useful insights into student understanding. Another was on strategies for using technology for entrance slips and quick quizzes.

In other schools, teachers asked for more information on deconstructing large-scale standards into measurable learning outcomes so that students could track progress. And some wanted opportunities to work collaboratively to design sequences of learning and align assessments. There is no best way to achieve this. Here are some questions to consider in your local practice of sequenced and cyclical assessment:

1. In what ways are your standards, goals, and learning targets clear and aligned? What are some areas for improvement?
2. How do you use pre-assessment to inform teaching, learning, and assessing?
3. How do you engage learners in achieving the targets?
4. What types of formative assessments do you embed in teaching and learning?
5. How do you utilize and respond to the data and insights from your formative assessments?

6. In what other ways do you use assessment to inform teaching and learning?
7. What do you need/want to learn more about to be an effective assessor?
8. What steps do you want to plan and/or act upon in charting a path to improvement?

Reciprocal and Responsive Assessment

Over the years, it feels as if I have learned more from my students than they have from me. It was humbling when Tashi described her experience trekking through the Himalayas to leave conflict in her own country. Marshall told of being dropped off in Los Angeles with an "uncle" who turned out to be a homeless alcoholic. He had to fend for himself at age 14 until a family services worker discovered him.

What I realize from these students is that learning goes beyond mastering content. It goes right into the heart and soul of children who are receptive and grateful for the support and assistance they receive. For me, this awareness means that as teachers, we must stretch beyond the usual pattern of determining what students have learned from the teacher into the realm of what teachers can learn from their students. In this way students and teachers learn together in a reassuring and safe atmosphere and sometimes in unexpected ways.

Reciprocal Give and Take

When Tashi was assigned a research project, she chose the topic of gender inequality. While her language skills were developing quickly, most of the literature on this topic is written at higher academic levels. With some assistance selecting articles at a more feasible level of language, she was able to complete the project and present a persuasive argument to the class. Her EQ was highly developed and her IQ was more than adequate. With some assistance with language, she was able to convey the dire situation of women around the globe to the class. Her classmates had little understanding of the problem and thus the reciprocity was from student to student as well as from student to teacher.

The assessment of her project was based on a rubric for depth and elaboration of content; logical and purposeful progression of information; acquisition, evaluation, and synthesis of resources; creative design and production; and use of technology. With a slight adjustment to the use of technology, she achieved at the highest level and went on to present her work at a statewide competition.

Reciprocal Deconstruction

While the teacher is striving to build mastery of a large-scale standard, reciprocity means deconstructing the standard so the student can discover meaning and find sticky ways to support learning. Big picture standards can be deconstructed into a content area learning target. For example "write informative/explanatory texts to examine a topic and convey ideas, concepts, and inform-ation through the selection, organization, and analysis of relevant content." Subparts of this standard, in brief, require students to introduce a topic, develop the topic, use appropriate transitions, use precise language, and provide a concluding statement.

The big picture standards can be personalized and differen-tiated for the student by emphasizing vocabulary, or paragraph structure, or synthesis of ideas. This provides the flexibility for a reciprocal and mutual writing process. Together, the teacher, student, and peers, can identify misunderstandings and learning gaps. They can then offer supportive feedback and recommend fine-tuning so that the student can take ownership of their next steps.

This is in full alignment with the ideas of Richard Kellough and Noreen Kellough (1999), who explain that "teaching and learning are reciprocal processes that depend on and affect one another. Thus, the assessment component deals with how well the students are learning and how well the teacher is teaching" (p. 417).

Responding to Assessment

In Chapter 2 we will look at formative assessment and the insights into learning that come from these embedded strategies. But, responsiveness goes beyond that. It means planning for expected outcomes as well as unexpected ones.

In relation to pre-assessment and using knowledge of students' entry level knowledge and skills it means:

1. Deciding the response triggers: when is it most important to take action.
2. Making connections to students' prior experiences/learning to develop a comfort level with the new learning.
3. Adjusting the sequence, content, and resources for the lesson.

During learning, as the students' strengths and challenges become increasingly visible it means:

1. Varying learning activities or mode of delivery.
2. Splitting up or chunking dense material into smaller steps or subparts.
3. Adjusting the pacing and depth of learning.
4. Using think-alouds to make learning visible.
5. Supporting students as self-assessors.

After learning:

1. Use multiple indicators of achievement.
2. Verify that assessments are valid, reliable, and fair for all learners.
3. Offer choice and differentiation in assessment methods.
4. Respond to patterns and trends in individual and whole class learning outcomes.
5. Consider adjustments to curriculum, resources, and assessments.

Unexpected Outcomes

Although all teachers are required to teach to standards, there are ways to accomplish this that extends learning beyond the standards.

Students in Mrs. Falana's class were reading a story about people who were doing good deeds but didn't want anyone to know who they were. They watched "Pay it Forward" as part of their unit on character development.

As it happened, the previous year the school had eliminated the honor roll assembly. The class thought it would be a good idea to have a character honor roll that was accessible to all students, not only the top academic achievers. Ms. Falana recognized that project-based learning was just the right match for the required literacy standards.

The students began by identifying positive character traits, then defining them and describing how someone would show them. They designed a checklist for the traits and also a criteria guide for their selection of students who demonstrated these traits. As in the story, the class did not want to be recognized for their actions, so they recruited the assistant principal to help them. They then designed a large character board for display in the school foyer. It included an explanation of character and behaviors that displayed good character. After taking an "oath of invisibility," they paid extra attention to students' behaviors during the school day, and at the end of each week brought a list of positive actions they saw classmates displaying. A code number was given to each candidate by the teacher who was the only one who knew all their names.

The class discussed, analyzed, and evaluated students' behaviors, actions, and words based on the criteria. They used a questioning protocol and then class members anonymously cast their vote with an explanation of their reasoning. Reading, viewing, and writing about other people who also demonstrated the trait was a required part of the project. As the year went on, and students in the school began to realize the value of good character, more names continued to be added to the board. Not only did the students in the class recognize what character traits looked like in practice, they also learned about people who persevered (Michael Jordan), showed compassion (Mother Teresa), and made the world a better place (Eleanor Roosevelt).

At the end of the year, when almost everyone had earned a spot on the character board, they presented their projects on famous, or in some cases, not so famous, individuals who are making or who have made the world a better place through their big or small actions. Madeline made a poster about her grandfather, a war veteran; Tomassa shared about her adopted brother who overcame many challenges in his life; and Reagan wrote a poem about a neighbor who collected food and raised money for the local food pantry. Students presented their individual projects using various media. The whole class learned about Paul Lauterbur who invented MRI; James Watson and Francis Crick for their double helix model of DNA; Nelson Mandela for ending Apartheid; Mozart; Socrates; Da Vinci and more.

The projects were assessed with a rubric that matched the assignment criteria. They were self-assessed with an accompanying narrative that included strategies for improvement, as well as peer and teacher feedback and review.

In Practice

There is a body of research on reciprocal teaching as an instructional activity where students become the teacher in a small group reading session through questioning, clarifying, and predicting. However there is not much information on the bigger picture ideas in this section on responsive and reciprocal learning and assessment. The research on lateral topics that are cited throughout this book support these key ideas and critical actions:

- ◆ Clarity of learning targets and purpose for learning.
- ◆ Availability of exemplars.
- ◆ Manageable steps and subgoals.
- ◆ Student engagement in determining process and product of learning.
- ◆ Supporting students as meaning-makers.
- ◆ Emotional connections to learning.
- ◆ Routine use of formative assessment and feedback.
- ◆ Self- and peer assessment.
- ◆ Using/applying learning in real-world situations.
- ◆ Gradual release of responsibility.

Checkpoint on Reciprocal and Responsive Assessment

Select three from the list and consider the connections you can make in your setting to link the research to your current practices in teaching, learning, and assessing. Then think about modifications you would like to mend.

Examples

1. *Research*: Manageable steps and subgoals. I will deconstruct the standards into assessable chunks then vary the learning activities and adjust the pacing in response to students' indications of understanding and analysis. I will work with small groups to support their mastery while monitoring patterns in whole class learning.

2. *Practice*: I realize the importance of letting students know what they will be learning, how they will be learning it, what they are expected to do with their learning, and how their learning outcomes will be assessed. But sometimes I find that the large-scale standards are too big for students to understand and deconstruct. I need to give some thought to making the standards comprehensible.

3. *Action*: In my unit on (add any topic or text) I need to make sure that I get their attention from the start by helping them make a personal connection to the topic and supporting them in constructing links between various parts of the text with ideas outside the text.

Chapter Summary

Key Ideas

1. Transparency of standards and methods is essential to improved learning outcomes.
2. Precisely aligned assessments help learners deepen learning.

3. Assessment is a constructive process that contributes to learning.

4. Deconstruct content so that assessments align with targeted chunks of learning.

5. Assessment is most effective when it is implemented as part of a continuous cycle.

6. Blending teaching, learning, and assessing increases instructional productivity.

7. Responding to purposeful and aligned assessment strengthens learning outcomes.

8. Supporting students as assessors is a valuable learning strategy.

Why This Works

Humans are not always fully purposeful beings, but rather we are driven by complex systems of emotions, relationships, genetic influences, and occasionally rational behavior. It is the rational part of our brains, the prefrontal cortex, that helps us plan our path in purposeful ways (Donoso, Collins, and Koechlin, 2014). It is this part of our brain that thoughtfully analyzes feedback on our actions and behaviors and helps us consider whether to do it again the same way, or try something different. Learners need feedback that makes it safe to make mistakes, helps them understand their misunderstandings, and provides opportunities for improvement.

Assessment comes in many forms. This can make it a little daunting when selecting strategies and interpreting measures. As informed educators we must rely on scientifically grounded information that provides the best evidence of success. Using proven practices, teachers and learning communities can examine the results, analyze the outcomes, and determine responses.

In relation to teaching, it makes more sense for your evaluator to provide feedback based on clear performance criteria, such as "Try counting to five after asking a question to allow students to think before responding." It makes little sense for you or them to tell the learner to simply "try harder." For example, you may be told to try a longer wait time after asking a question or to check that your test questions contain similar vocabulary to your learning targets. On the other hand, if they simply tell you to try harder, you may not rely on this person the next time you have a problem. This reciprocal nature of assessment works at all levels and guides continuous improvement even for the most challenging students.

Reflection and Application

Individual Reflection

Assess your own purposeful assessment using this checklist.

Rate each on a 4 to 1 scale:

4 = I have strong skills on this indicator.
3 = My skills are acceptable with some room for growth.
2 = I will endeavor to build stronger knowledge and skills.
1 = I am just at the beginning of my learning and skill building.

___ I understand the purpose of aligned and symbiotic assessments.

___ I feel confident in my ability to align instruction with assessment.

___ I am able to design a comprehensive, sequential, yet feasible unit of study.

___ I use pre-assessments to adjust my planning in response to student's incoming knowledge and skills.

___ My assessments are designed to align with the learning targets.

___ I routinely use multiple measures to assess learning.

___ I am able to interpret the assessment data to understand strengths and gaps.

___ I use a range of strategies to respond to assessment data.

Table 1.9 Growth Plan

In relation to purposeful, planned, and aligned assessment what do you want to learn more about or utilize in your school or classroom?	Describe current practices and level of knowledge.	Upskilling: What will you do to learn more? How will you apply it? What do you hope to achieve?

Professional Learning Group Reflection

Table 1.10 Where Are We Now? Where Do We Want to Be?

	ASSESSMENT STRATEGIES i.e., Large-scale, common, performance selected choice	WHAT DO THEY ALIGN WITH i.e., Mission, standards, curriculum	WHY DO WE USE THEM? i.e., Grading, interventions, reporting	WHO USES THEM Teacher, community, administrator, students
CURRENT				
CHANGES WE WANT TO MAKE				

2

Informative Assessment

Objectives of this chapter

1. Incorporate clear and visible targets and assessments into teaching and learning.
2. Use assessment purposefully to inform teaching and support learning.
3. Value and rely on assessment as an essential source of insight into student learning.
4. Prepare and analyze assessments with an emphasis on growth and improvement.

Assessment for Learning/Learning from Assessment

If you have an aching back it makes no sense to be diagnosed with a muscle sprain and then offered no treatment plan. Too often in education, students are tested and scores reported. Sometimes the scores aren't available for some time after the test. Other times, the tests are returned expediently and the whole class moves on to the next unit as scheduled in the curriculum map.

Assessment that is used informatively is similar to an X-ray or MRI that informs a diagnosis for an individual patient. In the classroom, informative assessments guide teachers' decisions.

When Ms. Moran begins a new unit on adding three digit numbers she gives everyone the same pretest then identifies students who understand place value and regrouping and those who are having difficulty with it. She then groups the students into those who need direct instruction, those who need practice, and those who are ready to move forward. In using assessment this way, students and teachers strategically assess knowledge and skills, use this information to purposefully guide decisions, and focus on improvement and growth.

Clear Learning Targets

When something is visible it can be seen clearly, sometimes from close-up or perhaps from a distance. Occasionally there is glare and parts of the image are reflected away. At other times looking through the mist can make things indistinct. Objects can be seen clearly when the glare and fog are removed and the details become clear, from both near and far.

According to Webster's Dictionary, synonyms for visible include recognizable, evident, obvious, and accessible. Visible assessment occurs when students know the learning outcomes and how they will be assessed. Teachers link the assessments to instructional purposes enabling them to see the outcomes of learning through their students' eyes. In this way, both sides of the teaching/learning process are visible and purposeful.

Mr. Warren uses a common assessment that all the fifth grade teachers are required to use. It mirrors the standardized test in that it includes primarily selected choice questions with a few completion items.

He deconstructs the standard "graph points on the coordinate plane to solve real-world and mathematical problems." He begins by showing them examples of this concept in practice such as the game Battleship and BrainPop's "Game Over Gopher."

He wants to raise the level of engagement as well as the depth of thinking so prior to the grade-level test he has his students label the x and y axis on graph paper and then count and mark every fifth line. Since it is near Halloween, he asks them to draw a haunted house on their paper. Each student labels 10 points on their drawing and in groups of three review each other's labeling. He circulates and checks their work.

He then has students write word problems for a variety of graphed images. His examples include "If you wanted to enter the front door by ringing the door bell, where would you start?" He reviews their submissions for accuracy as well as errors. Just before distributing a quickie quiz he reviews the common mistakes he identified in the word problems they wrote.

In scoring the classroom quiz, he notices one more common error and reviews that with the whole class before administering the common assessment. At this point he is pretty confident that his students will do well on the common assessment. When they do, they have a 5 minute dance party to the Cha Cha Slide.

Visible Outcomes

Anderson and Krathwohl (2001) explain that students are more apt to be successful when they know the learning targets. In addition, if they know the outcomes and types of measures they can better regulate their study and learning strategies. It makes a difference when they know whether they are expected to memorize the regions of the United States or to explain the influence of regional differences on people's life styles.

Visible assessment is like priming the well. Students can see the water source. They understand how they will be retrieving the water and how much they are expected to get into their container. By using assessment norms and routines, students are better aware of the expectations. When the element of surprise is removed students are more confident in their ability to be successful.

Whether introducing a new concept or preparing students for a test, there is comfort in knowing where they are headed and what is expected. Sometimes a test can take a student by complete surprise. One student told me his final exam had nothing to do with the year's-worth of learning in that the teacher told the students to pick an era of history and write 26 facts about it using each of the letters of the alphabet. For the letter Z she wrote "The Civil War battles reminded me of the movie *World War Z*." She received credit for that answer. But the teacher received minimal insight into her learning.

It is far better to provide or have students develop the test review, and even better, have them write test questions. Relying on the test blueprint described in Chapter 1, the standards are visible, the learning targets are clear, and the assessment strategies are known.

In Practice: Clear Thoughts

In Mr. Cabrini's seventh grade science class, the students are studying plate tectonics. In relation to the large-scale standards, students "determine the meaning of symbols, key terms, and other domain-specific words and phrases as they are used in scientific or technical context" and the Science Standard of "analyze and interpret data on the distribution of fossils and rocks, continental shapes, and seafloor structures to provide evidence of the past plate motions." He recognizes that this educational language would be unclear to his students so he deconstructs this into more straightforward and measurable outcomes.

Students will:

1. state and describe the cause of tectonic plate movement (*Remember*);
2. recognize different types of plate boundaries such as transverse, convergent, and divergent (*Understand*);
3. draw and label each layer of the earth. Write two facts about that layer such as its thickness, composition, temperature, etc. (*Apply*); and
4. evaluate the accuracy of Alfred Wegener's Theory of tectonic plates (*Evaluate*).

For each learning objective students are asked related questions.

Objective #:

1. The heat from the outer and inner core warm up magma that rises to the crust and begins to cool. This is known as convection currents. ____True ____ False

2. Write the names of the boundary types shown in the picture below (Figure 2.1). _____

Figure 2.1 Boundary Plates

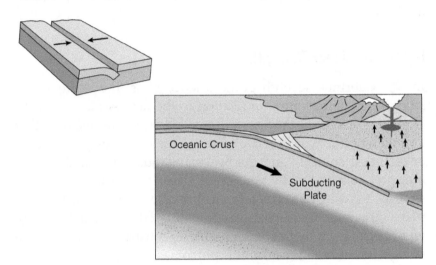

3. A blank image of a sphere (similar to Figure 2.2) is provided and an associated space to label record facts about each layer.

Figure 2.2 Layers of the Earth

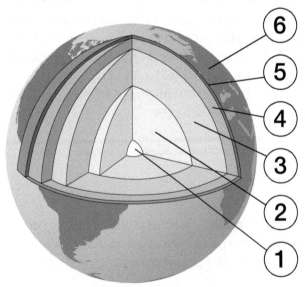

4. An image shown below, or a video of recent volcanic activity (one is available at pbslearningmedia), is provided with space to record a response about Wegener's theory.

Figure 2.3 Tectonic Plates and Volcanic Activity

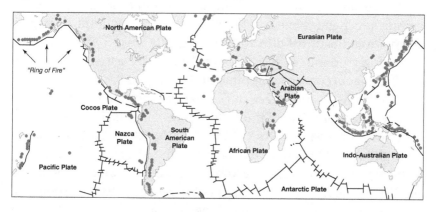

In this way there are no surprises for the students on the test and no surprises for the teacher on students' knowledge and skills.

Coherent Assessment

In the hands of a skilled teacher, in a student-focused classroom, assessment policies and practices are clear to the students from the first day. Assessments are also the means for reinforcing and embedding learning as well as making gaps apparent. In this way the day to day classroom assessments support, yet go beyond, the content measured by large-scale tests. Ms. Parisi provides a learning tracker for each unit of learning. In addition to including learning targets and activities, she identifies the assessment points with their weighting. Typically these describe homework assignments, weekly classroom check-ins, self/peer reviews, scoring of projects, and tests. When these are brought home and returned with a parent's signature, she is reassured that the process is visible to all her valued constituents.

When John Hattie (2009; 2011) published *Visible Learning* his synthesis of over 800 studies included an analysis of over 100 teaching practices that influence learning outcomes. His book has become a benchmark for high-quality teaching and learning. In subsequent publications he has helped educators understand which strategies are most effective and which have a minimal influence on learning. His summary of effect sizes has led to significant changes in educational practice. Many of the strategies he identified as most effective are strongly linked to assessment including students as self-assessors, formative assessment, effective feedback, concept mapping, and exemplars,

Robert Marzano's (2007) *The Art and Science of Teaching*, is another meta-analysis of multiple studies on effective instruction. It builds on his earlier work *What Works in Schools* (2003). In both, he explains and illustrates the most effective strategies for learning, understanding, and applying knowledge. In relation to assessment, his list includes clear learning goals, tracking student progress, effective feedback, high expectations, cohesive/aligned instruction and assessment, graphic representations of learning, effective questioning, generating and testing hypotheses, anticipatory set (a.k.a. pre-assessment), and checking for understanding.

In addition to Hattie's and Marzano's work, the research is wide and deep on best practice in assessment. Multiple expert sources inform us of this: National Research Council (2001), National Center for Research on Evaluation, Standards, and Student Testing, National Center for Improvement of Educational Assessment, Lorrie Shepard, Linda Darling-Hammond, James Pellegrino, Karin Hess, Dylan Wiliam, Margaret Heritage, and many more.

Selected high-yield strategies that emerge from the research are shown in Table 2.1. This is far from a comprehensive listing, but rather is based on top tier routines that are supported by assessment practices.

Please note; there are valuable strategies, but ones that are not solidly connected to assessment such as home environment, classroom management, resources, and relationships that are not included. This doesn't mean they are not important.

Table 2.1 Visible Assessment in Practice

Student actions	Teacher facilitation	Visible assessment strategy
Formative assessment	Embedded throughout teaching and learning	Assessment before, during, and after learning to inform students and teachers of progress and next steps
Student self-assessment	Reciprocal teaching and modeling of summarizing, questioning, inquiry	Explicit teaching of strategies and tools for self-assessment
Metacognitive strategies	Examining, questioning, clarifying, and explaining thoughts and actions	Prompts and strategies that probe learning and support reflection
Tracking progress	Ongoing monitoring of learning by teachers and students to identify progress and lingering gaps	Visible recording and analysis of learning using classroom learning trackers and data management programs
Graphic representations of learning	Various types of graphic organizers from paper and pencil to electronic	Multiple opportunities to sort and organize learning and show understanding
Feedback	Routine feedback that is specific, standards-based, actionable	Feedback: Teacher and peer emphasis on progress from prior to present to future learning
Cooperative learning	Purposeful grouping of students for teaching and learning	Guided collaboration with peer review and feedback. Targeted and responsive support
Engagement in learning	Student-centered teaching	Hands-on real-world connections between standards and application
Background knowledge/ Connections to prior learning	Pre-assessment	KWL's, pre-assessments, fact-checking incoming beliefs. Making meaning by building on prior learning
Mastery/ Standards-based learning Purposeful	Assessment	Clear learning goals, reasonable challenge, unambiguous success criteria with exemplars

When assessment is visible to students it means:

◆ students know the learning targets;
◆ they know how to achieve their goals;
◆ they routinely receive feedback on their work;
◆ progress and growth is emphasized;
◆ assessments offer real-world applications; and
◆ the assessment methods gain their attention and hold their interest.

Checkpoint on Coherent Assessment

As you read the chart on "Visible Assessment in Practice" ideas for applying best practice in visible assessment may have become apparent to you. Use Table 2.2 to select a couple that resonate with you and that you want to learn more about and/or apply in your daily practice.

Table 2.2 Checkpoint on Visible Assessment

Key idea: Describe how you currently use it.	What additional knowledge and skills do you need in order to use it more effectively?	Consider changes to your current practice to make your teaching more effective and student learning more visible.

Transparent To All

We've been talking about the importance of students knowing and understanding learning targets and the ways they will be measured. Keep in mind that standards and targets must also be visible to other constituents. Students and schools are best served when all these groups work collectively and transparently.

Whether standards and targets are local or large-scale they must be visible and accessible:

- ◆ at the policy level;
- ◆ for state education departments;
- ◆ to schools and districts;
- ◆ by educational organizations;
- ◆ for resource developers;
- ◆ in local communities; and
- ◆ to parents.

In addition ensure that:

- ◆ targets are clearly written and understandable for a variety of audiences;
- ◆ assessment processes, procedures, uses and users are transparent;
- ◆ evidence of learning is displayed in ways that are comprehensible to all parties;
- ◆ a balanced spectrum of strategies support a range of learning outcomes; and
- ◆ data is presented in plain language so the results have meaning to constituents.

Classroom and students are the ones for whom the standards must be written. When a teacher reads "conduct short as well as more sustained research projects to answer a question (including a self-generated question) or solve a problem; narrow or broaden the inquiry when appropriate; synthesize multiple sources on the subject, demonstrating understanding of the subject under investigation" it is not always easy to figure out how to teach and assess it, as this big picture standard doesn't describe the type of research, the steps to take, how to monitor progress, or assess the outcomes.

The most important place for standards to be visible and actionable is the classroom. When standards are used by teachers and their students here's what they need to know.

- **Where am I headed**: Before instruction
  What am I aiming for?
  How can I get there?
  What are the final expectations?
  What are the final measures: growth or a specific score?
- **How can I get there**: During learning
  How am I doing?
  Am I on the right path?
  Am I making progress?
  What if it's not working?
- **How will I know**: After learning
  How did I do?
  How can I show you what I learned?
  What do I still need to know and do?

In a transparent educational system learning targets are visible; evidence of learning is continuously collected, scrutinized, and shared; and progress is clearly communicated. In this way, assessment becomes collaborative and supports students in achieving their best outcomes.

Reflection on Visible Assessment

Professional learning community discussion question

Formative assessment has a more than adequate amount of quality research to utilize it as an effective assessment practice. Additional ideas for making assessment visible were described in this section.

1. Think, pair, and share with your professional learning group the strategies you believe are most important or best suited to your specific practice.
2. Discuss how you can advance, develop, and improve their use in classrooms.
3. Identify any barriers you may encounter and consider strategies for overcoming them.

In Practice: Visible Assessment

Standards

Add and subtract within 1,000, using concrete models or drawings and strategies based on place value, properties of operations, and/or the relationship between addition and subtraction; relate the strategy to a written method. Understand that in adding or subtracting three-digit numbers, one adds or subtracts hundreds and hundreds, tens and tens, ones and ones; and sometimes it is necessary to compose or decompose tens or hundreds.

Local Curriculum Goal

Students will read and write three and four digit numbers using place value understanding. They will use expanded, standard, and word form when working with numbers.

Classroom Learning Objective

Students can read, write, understand, and apply to word problems, numbers within 1,000.

Student Learning Targets

I will add and subtract numbers within 1,000.
I will complete work problems using numbers within 1,000.
I will explain to someone else how to solve a work problem that requires addition and subtraction within 1,000.
I will track my learning from the pre-assessment to the post-test.

Teaching and Learning

Pretest sample questions

Question 1: What number makes the equation true?

$$244 + \_\_\_\_ = 239 + 7$$

Question 2: Write the subtraction sentence (equation) that fits the story: Edgar counted six hundred thirty-seven people at the big game where everyone wore their team's shirts. 247 wore brown "bears' team" shirts. How many wore yellow "ducks' team" shirts?

In response to the pretest she starts with a whole class learning activity on place value, then follows-up with individual and small group learning using Learn Zillion and Front Row so that students can progress at their own rate with numerical and word problems. Her school has clickers so she can quickly and easily monitor students' responses to questions.

Assessments

Formative strategies and feedback engage students in solving problems, devising problems, playing math games, and explaining it to visitors from Planet Xenon.

At the conclusion, students self-assess their learning using the following scale that they were given at the start of the unit. This time they are asked to include an example of what they know and can do with their self-assessment of each learning target.

1. I can read numbers up to 1,000 but not sure I write them correctly.
2. I can read and write numbers in standard form such as 425.
3. I can read and write numbers in standard and written form: 425 and four hundred twenty-five.
4. I can read and write numbers up to 1,000 in three ways.
5. I can read, write, and solve word problems using numbers greater than 1,000.

Formative Assessment

I have always thought that the term formative assessment would be better expressed through the word informative. Although formative has its basis in the Latin *formare* meaning to form, it is routinely used in developmental literature to describe growth and maturation. On the other hand, informative has its roots in the Latin word *informare* and was used in relation to instructing and guiding the formation of something or someone. To avoid confusion in this section, the term formative will be used to describe the ideas that have emerged, developed, and taken shape from the work of Michael Scriven (1967) who first distinguished formative from summative in relation to goals, strategies, and use.

Jeffrey Karpicke (2012) found that studying something over and over such as memorizing vocabulary or a sequence of events has little effect on long-term retention. More importantly, he found that repeated assessments, embedded throughout learning, served to bolster long-term learning. This process of ongoing active retrieval is fully supportive of formative assessment and corresponds with the basic tenets of quality assessment: alignment with learning targets, routine checking-ins to gauge growth, engagement of learners, and purposeful responses. In this way, assessment begins before teaching begins rather than when a student hands in his or her final work.

Formative Processes

Contemporary authorities who have translated theory into practice include Paul Black and Dylan Wiliam (2009), Linda Darling-Hammond (2014), Rick Stiggins (2005), Margaret Heritage (2010), James Popham (2008), and Lorrie Shepard (2000; 2005). Definitions vary in length from one sentence to whole chapters. A summary of their essential elements of formative assessment include:

- explicit learning outcomes;
- clear and visible criteria for success;
- evidence of learning elicited throughout teaching and learning;
- students engaged in goal setting and assessment of achievement;
- assessments are purposefully embedded throughout instruction;
- descriptive feedback identifies strengths, gaps, and strategies for improvement;
- teaching is responsive through adjustments to instruction, academic support, resources, pacing, grouping, etc.; and
- the assessment cycle is enduring and continues throughout teaching and learning.

Checkpoint on Formative Process

How would you summarize these ideas into a statement of 30 words or less (basically, this is a generous tweet)?

_____ _____ _____ _____ _____ _____ _____

_____ _____ _____ _____ _____ _____ _____

_____ _____ _____ _____ _____ _____ _____

_____ _____ _____ _____ _____ _____ _____

_____ _____

Here's one exemplar for comparing your definition:

> "Formative assessment is a process used by teachers and students during instruction that provides feedback to adjust ongoing teaching and learning to improve students' achievement of intended instructional outcomes."
>
> (CCSSO, 2012)

Formative Practice

There is enough research and information on formative assessment to fill a vault. Yet, studies show that it is used inconsistently by teachers (Marshall and Drummond, 2006). In some classrooms it is a spur of the moment activity to see if students are paying attention, other times it may be a quick check-in by a teacher when she perceives blank stares or confused faces. Some teachers believe formative practice to be the use of off-the-shelf interim and benchmark assessment. In reality, it is not the strategy but rather the purpose, placement, and response that make it informative and valuable.

In relation to purpose, formative strategies can identify incoming knowledge, display progress, probe for higher level thinking, and summarize learning. In relation to placement, formative strategies can be used before, during, and after teaching and learning such as to pre-assess, check on progress, or summarize learning. Responding to formative assessment means adjusting teaching strategies, resources, pacing, timing, and grouping.

Formative for a Purpose

In Chapter 1, we considered the value of purposefully planned and aligned assessment. In this section we will take a deeper look into those concepts as they relate to formative assessment.

Taking a sample of incoming knowledge is like checking the ingredients before you begin cooking. It is important to the quality of the final product to have all the necessary ingredients available from the start or alternatively make a quick stop at the grocery store to refill the pantry. This type of previewing lays a foundation for starting the process of learning on the best route that will lead to the goal.

It is essential for learners to build on the right foundations, for example, learning addition before multiplication or molecular structure before covalent bonding. A minute quiz at the beginning of class can reveal this knowledge. Alternatively, a strategy such as predicting what they will learn in the lesson or unit can also be illuminating. One teacher who asked what students should be learning in their study of planets received the response: "I really want to learn how to build a rocket to send my sister to Jupiter." The next time she pre-assessed, she used a previewing strategy with three prompts about the planets:

1. Name one planet and tell two facts you know about it. Consider color, location, surface, gravity, etc. (Knowledge)
2. Which of these planets would be most apt to sustain life and why do you think so? Mercury, Mars, Neptune. (Understanding)
3. Describe 3 ways you could get to Jupiter—be creative. (Generating new ideas)

Ms. Mazore has a very active third grade class this year. She purposefully searches for formative strategies that will keep them engaged during teacher-directed learning. As she explains cause and effect she includes examples and demonstrates key concepts. Then the students record, with words or pictures, their own ideas on why someone is shivering while dressed in summer clothes, or predict what will happen next in illustrations of catapults. This type of tracking of learning and thinking beyond what is being said or shown serves as a reminder to students of the context of learning in addition to the content. It also provides a visible record for the teacher of student understanding.

Formative assessment also supports collaborative learning. During a unit on poetry, Mrs. Moore sets up a team challenge. Each team of 3 students writes a brief poem using one of the types they have been studying in class: haiku, cinquain, shape poem, free form. The poems are traded and each group analyzes the poem against quality indicators. Each of the groups report out and receive feedback. In this way students lead the review and the teacher can clarify any lingering misunderstandings.

Reflection on Formative Purpose

A critical element of best practice in assessment is that it is designed or selected for a purpose. Consider these questions in determining your rationale in selecting a strategy:

◆ What is the best way to gather the informative information? Does questioning provide adequate evidence of learning or would it be better to have students record or demonstrate their work in another way?

◆ What do you intend to glean from the formative strategy? Are you looking for content knowledge, higher level thinking, or application of learning?

◆ How much time do you want to spend in relation to the purpose? Are there ways that quick signaling such as holding up answer cards or using *Plickers* (a useful classroom app) works as well as a group problem solving activity?

◆ Perhaps it is not the content and application of learning that is a problem but the pacing, sequence, and resources. How can you find out more about those important influences on learning and make necessary adjustments?

Formative by Placement

If every child had an academic GPS we would know at all times where they are in their learning. Without that technology (yet) there are many strategies that teachers and students can use to check on progress. No manager would, nor teacher should, give up in the middle of the game because their team was behind. Rather, they scrutinize the errors, identify gaps in practice, and select the right time to call a meeting on the mound.

From Socrates' use of questions to the contemporary work of Kathleen Cotton (1988), Douglas Fuchs and Nancy Fuchs (2002), and OECD/CERI (2008), the value of tracking and monitoring learning to guide instructional decisions and provide feedback to learners has been proven. In addition, it is important to select the right strategy at the right moment.

Formative assessment is built on these foundational concepts: clarify where students are at the start of learning, where they are headed during learning, and how they are progressing towards the goal. It is the purposeful placement and response to formative assessment at the just-right time and place that supports this process.

Ms. Chema learned this through trial and error when she began teaching a unit based on the district curriculum with its accompanying lesson plans. She started out by explaining latitude and longitude, Greenwich Mean Time, and the design of a 24-hour clock. When she asked the students to solve time-zone word problems, the class fell apart. Although they listened attentively, they had no background knowledge on the new material she was teaching them.

She quickly devised a short quiz to determine their incoming knowledge. Three simple questions about the direction of latitude and longitude, the students' own time zones, and their travel experiences revealed minimal understanding. It took a little searching for Ms. Chema to find a globe, a light bulb, and a toy airplane, along with a 24-hour online clock. By the next morning she had developed a learning tracker for them to record these emerging understandings. But as she explained, she wouldn't have been able to do that without the information gleaned from the pre-assessment.

Mr. Quimby was at the end of the unit on the civilizations of Egypt, Greece, and Rome when he had a similar "aha!" moment. He used a question and answer mix-up where each student wrote a short answer test question on blue paper and the answer to their question on green paper. He collected the green ones and randomly redistributed them. When a student read their question, the person with the answer would hold it up and read it for the question writer to confirm or deny, at which time the answerer could phone a friend who thought they had the right answer card. The review went well, misconceptions were clarified, and students seemed ready for the unit test.

Following this informative and engaging student-led review, Mr. Quimby distributed the test that all the grade level teachers were using. As he monitored the test he noticed lots of consternation on students' faces. In response, he decided to ask the students to post up to three questions that they thought were the hardest to answer. As he considered them, he realized that many students didn't understand the term "cultural diffusion." During his test walk-about he noticed that students had narrowed the choices down to two possibilities with the correct one being that the Nile prevented cultural diffusion. When he clarified the meaning of cultural diffusion, using an example from prior classwork, faces lit up and half the students changed their answer to the correct one before turning in their test. In this case it was a lack of vocabulary rather than a lack of understanding of the subject matter. In this way, a wisely placed review during the summative assessment can lead to more accurate assessment of learning.

Appropriate placement of formative assessment supports effective monitoring during teaching and learning. This in turn guides informed responses to the data generated by the assessments. This is the time and place when the teacher decides what and how to adjust content, pacing, depth, resources, grouping, or learning activities.

Checkpoint on Formative Strategies

A few additional formative strategies are described here. Consider how and when you would adapt and use each of them.

1. Use graphic organizers or paper links for students to explain how new learning connects to prior learning.
2. During learning, students color code their work to align with the learning targets. Gaps in teaching and learning become evident prior to the summative test.
3. From–To: Students record their thinking on how a big picture idea converts to a local action, or how a general concept is applied to a specific practice.
4. Questioning Volleyball: Rather than asking a question and calling on a student, have students respond to another student's answer by reflecting on it, clarifying it, asking another question, or passing it on to another student for further exploration.
5. Split Judgment: Write a claim on the left and evidence to support or refute it on the right.
6. Fix it: Students are given a review sheet or study questions that have all the answers wrong. They recalculate, correct, or explain the error.
7. Humpty Dumpty Summary: In small groups, students are given parts of a sequence or story to reassemble in the correct configuration.
8. I used to think____, but now I know____: Students clarify and explain their new learning in relation to prior knowledge.

Reflection on Formative Assesment

How will you select an assessment that aligns with your purpose? Where will you use it in the teaching/learning process? Record some ideas in the grid below. (See Table 2.3, p. 70.)

Assessment that Illuminates

Formative and summative assessments have a complex symbiotic relationship. They inform both the teacher and the learner by providing evidence of learning. More than a side dish or add-on

Table 2.3 Reflection on Formative Assessment

Purpose	Learning target	Formative assessment strategy/placement
Review and extend prior learning	Students will describe traits of multiple characters in the story	Brainstorm as many character traits as we can. Each student gets one trait to look up, define, and explain to the class. At the beginning of learning

at the end of teaching and learning, assessment belongs right in the center of the plateful of skills and knowledge, diffusing in all directions from the appetizer to the main course and all the way through dessert. In this way assessment changes from a trimming like parsley to a strategy like slow-cooking for supporting, informing, and improving learning.

Teachers and students need to know the inputs, pathways, and outcomes of learning as well as how those outcomes will be judged, interpreted, and utilized. To do this, teachers must be prepared and empowered to routinely gather evidence of learning in the classroom and then analyze, reflect, and respond to it. Students must also be equipped to substantiate learning, identify strengths and weaknesses, and try alternative solutions. In this way informative assessment is a symbiotic, reciprocal, and illuminating process.

Assessment that Supports Learners

Throughout learning, students need to see the goal lines and continuously check on whether they are heading in the right direction, at the right pace, and whether there are obstructions that might impede their progress. Assessment is what happens throughout their learning rather than just their score at the end of the game.

Students use teacher, peer, and self-assessment to drill down for deeper understanding. In doing so, they can more clearly define what they need to know, how they can learn it, and how it applies to real life. This in turn, guides them in organizing, synthesizing, and producing more purposefully.

John Hattie (2009) found that setting standards and using them for self-judgment has a strong effect size of .62. When students use a checklist before turning in work or compare their work to exemplars, they can use this to improve learning outcomes. Feedback and routine check-ins help students make sense of their progress in reaching towards big ideas. When they are asked to add more supporting details to their work, they can raise the quality of their work.

The Value of Feedback

When I drive to an unfamiliar place, even when my GPS is on, I wonder if I am heading in the right direction, how far along the route I am, and how much longer to my destination. I know I've arrived when a picture of the destination shows up on my screen. At times, feedback is very exacting such as "Remember to move the decimal point 2 places to the left when converting a percentage." Other times it is more of a strategy for improvement, such as "Add more details to your definition of a community as it is more than the name of a town." If my GPS said "good job" but I was in the wrong place, it wouldn't be helpful in correcting my route.

Feedback is intended to be given while there is still time to navigate learning by seeking more reliable directions or changing course. "Feedback is one of the most powerful influences on learning and achievement" (Hattie and Timperley, 2007, p. 81). This opening statement of their report is then tempered by their explanation that the impact can be positive or negative depending on its substance. Avraham Kluger and Angelo DeNisi (1996) also found that feedback can have inconsistent outcomes depending on the task, the quality of feedback, and the type of personalization. Both researchers explain the qualities that make it most effective and how it can be best used to promote success in the classroom. Valerie Shute (2007) provides a useful review of best practice. Below is a summary of the main ideas along with an example in the classroom.

1. Maintain focus on the target and task.
   "Your hypothesis is relevant. Now try to rewrite it as an 'if . . . then . . .' statement."

2. Provide feedback as close to the learning as possible. Clarify vocabulary during a learning activity rather than at the time of a test review.

3. Clearly describe achievement and gaps.
   "Accurate summary of the three main points, now add supportive details to them."

4. Be specific to the student's work.
   "You followed the correct procedure but made a mathematical error in step 2 that you can correct and then recalculate."

5. Inform the learner of their next steps.
   "You included two accurate facts about the writers of the Declaration of Independence. Research and add one more: Please resubmit for additional credit."

6. Guide and support self-regulation.
   "It looks like you worked hard on this, but be sure to include all the information required in the assignment."

7. Response is timely in relation to the task and next steps.
   "Before you add your trusses, strengthen the supports."

8. Comments are comprehensible and actionable by the student.
   "Hold both hands up, backs facing you, point only your pointer (first) finger up. Then point your thumb to the side. Whichever one is in the shape of an L is your left. Turn towards that hand."

9. Advise the next steps of the teacher.
   If most students got Q. 4 wrong, consider why: Is it the question, the content, or the teaching?

Checkpoint on Feedback

How would you change each of these feedback statements to improve their quality?

Next time write more. _____

This doesn't look like your best effort. _____

Well, that didn't work out as expected: Now what? _____

Learning From Mistakes

I don't know about you, but my best learning has come from the times I burned the dinner, completely missed the tee, fell off a bicycle, and failed an economics exam. Most learning, as it works its way into our brain, passes through the amygdala. This tiny organ within the limbic system, translates sensory information into feelings and actions. It is only when we stop a moment before acting recklessly or speaking thoughtlessly, that our responses are monitored through our frontal cortex, the rational and contemplative part of our brain.

Due to the power of the emotional centers of the brain we are more apt to remember thrilling stories and eerie events rather than math formulas or lists of presidents. This is also why our feelings about ourselves and others influence our achievement. This is especially true for children and adolescents who have a more active emotional part of the brain and a less active rational portion. They may choose not to do their work because they don't like something the teacher said, or had a spat with a friend who was placed in their group, or are having a bad day because of a problem at home.

For all of us, young and old, a constant barrage of messages about our incompetence and ineptness leads to feelings of frustration and despair. This in turn leads to a loss of hope and unwillingness to try. This is especially true in today's world where so much comes so easily and instantly to children. Yet, achievement comes from a willingness not only to make mistakes but to learn from them. Maybe this tells us that it is more important to greet a wrong answer as a pathway to the right one. Perhaps this means we should embrace progress and growth rather than final scores. Consider Oscar Wilde's words in your classroom: "Experience is simply the name we give our mistakes."

Carol Dweck's (2008) work at Stanford on mindset has provided insights into this topic. She gave two groups of students a test of knowledge. When children received their scores, half were praised for being really smart and the other half were complimented for having worked really hard. When they were given a choice of their second test, the majority of students who were complimented for their effort chose the more challenging version. The children who were praised for being smart mostly chose the easy test. She describes students who have a growth mindset as those who are more willing to accept the idea of learning through mistakes and recognize the value of reasonable challenges. Children with a fixed mindset, who are regularly praised for any quality of work, are less apt to take a risk.

The neuroscientist turned teacher, Judy Willis (2014a), explains that personalizing learning, connecting it to prior learning, and actively engaging students in learning creates neural circuits that contribute to better memory. These positive experiences can support feelings of accomplishment, mastery of learning, and continuous progress. She also explains that overstimulation of the amygdala through high levels of stress actually block reasoning and memory storage.

Think about shifting your classes' outlook from "failure is not an option" to, as Thomas Edison said, "I haven't failed, I just found 10,000 ways that won't work." This means turning errors into learning opportunities that in turn, encourage students to be willing to take reasonable risks. One of my favorite videos is on the *Teaching Channel* and is called "My Favorite No." The teacher, Leah Alcala, poses a question at the start of class. Each student solves it on an index card and turns it in. She then quickly scans the cards for the most common errors, asks students for an explanation of collective mistakes, and supports them as they collaboratively clarify misunderstandings and make corrections. So simple, yet so effective.

Here are some recommendations for helping learners recognize the value of mistakes (you can personalize these ideas Table 2.4):

1. Start with small steps that involve the whole class. For example ask them to give directions for making a peanut butter and jelly sandwich then follow their directions *exactly* as you attempt to rip open the bag of bread or pound the jelly jar on the counter.

2. In your class, encourage extreme mistakes by having students make the worst paper airplane ever. Then analyze them and make suggestions for improvement. If you are going to assess growth, rather than using the final model that flew the farthest, use the student's design that showed the greatest improvement (in attitude, distance, or form) from the first attempt to the informed redesign.

3. Provide opportunities to practice new learning in a low risk setting such as collaboratively sorting books/stories into genres or hold a review session where students collectively record and summarize what they know.

4. Avoid cold calling. Instead cue students before they will be expected to answer a question. Be purposeful in the complexity of question you ask.

5. Share your own mistakes or errors in judgment.

6. Watch the YouTube video on "Famous Failures."

7. Teach your students about mindset; practice it, model it.

8. Take a "play break" during learning: play a game, tell jokes, dance, act silly.

9. Provide mild to moderate challenges and escalate the level of expectancy in response to students' demonstration of mastery. Start by building vocabulary, sort with a graphic organizer, and finally use the words in a story.

10. Teach through multiple modalities. Read, watch, act out weather, or even better, create clouds.

11. Provide opportunities to show learning in multiple ways: write, illustrate, show, or tell.

12. When giving a problem to be solved start by asking students to come up with the absolute wrong way to solve it.

13. When reviewing learning, let students call for a lifeline or "phone a friend" for support.

14. Students write what's hard about their new learning and what is easy. Clarify the common "hards" before the final assessment.

15. Give students opportunities to correct their mistakes that include an explanation of their new understanding in the process.

16. On a true/false test answer every question incorrectly. Then use source material to explain the right answer to a Martian (alternatively, just do this with the wrong answers when the test is returned).

17. After a test is returned to students, ask them to look up correct answers and record: I used to think____ but now I know____ because_____.

Table 2.4 Reflection on Learning from Mistakes

Strategy for learning from mistakes	How I would use it

18. Provide a grid for students where they can record the question(s) they got wrong and explain why: the question was too hard, the question was confusing, I made a simple mistake, I need more practice, I didn't study, etc.

19. Celebrate hard work but also, and especially, celebrate growth and improvement.

Reflection on Learning from Mistakes

Informs and Guides Instruction

Assessment is what guides and shapes instruction. Without knowing your incoming cooking skills, how would I know whether to teach you to peel a banana or to prepare bananas faster? How can a teacher know whether students are ready to move on to higher levels of math or deeper thinking about causes of war?

Students show learning in different ways. Matt and his group built the strongest bridge but could not mathematically illustrate the concepts. Morgan wrote a futuristic graphic novella but was failing English due to poor spelling. Henrietta produced a beautiful infographic classifying insects, but failed the unit test because she had difficulty memorizing.

It is important to assess all types of learning and to rely on a variety of strategies. Giving students multiple and diverse opportunities to show what they know results in the widest and most inclusive displays of their knowledge and abilities. All types of demonstrations of learning are informative. Sticky strategies such as empty outlines, sure/not sure, questioning, and summarizing all provide insights into learning. In turn, purposeful adjustments can be made to teaching and learning.

Everything is assessment: From determining a student's mood or mindset when they enter the classroom to seeing their eyes light up when they understand the irony of O. Henry. Assessment informs all levels of the decision-making loop: Policy, leadership, teachers, students, and parents. Assessment also informs a classroom culture where children learn that mistakes are okay, taking reasonable risks is acceptable, and monitoring learning is essential.

Improvement is most likely to occur when assessment and feedback supports learning through all layers and levels. Assessment is about helping students navigate rather than judging and sorting them. It is used by all constituents: it informs parents of targets and progress towards them; guides professional development; allocates resources; and informs new initiatives, school leadership, and educational structures.

In Practice

Mr. Delitto is in search of ways to use assessment informatively. He is beginning to incorporate more routine formative assessments, but isn't quite sure yet what to do about the information he gets from pre-assessments, displays of learning, and questioning. He invites a colleague, Mrs. Terry, to observe his class. They meet prior to review the lesson plan. His planned instructional strategy is a lecture on the Crusades and watching a few videos. His formative assessment is an empty outline where students fill in the words as Mr. Delitto lectures his class.

Mrs. Terry suggests he starts by posting the learning objectives and asking students what they know about each of them on an entry ticket where they can indicate their understanding of the locations, time frame, causes, controversies, and outcomes. She then observes the class and takes notes on the instructional practices and learning outcomes. She notices that although students are amenable to completing their empty outlines, they are not engaged in the learning. The content of the outline is directed at the mid-range student so while some are easily filling in the blanks, others are struggling to understand the vocabulary. When the tone sounds and the class ends, students put their papers in their binders.

They meet during their next planning period to talk about the lesson. Mr. Delitto finds his students easy to teach, compliant, and well behaved. In response to Mrs. Terry, he agrees that they are also somewhat apathetic. They discuss ways to check-in on learning before beginning a lesson and as students complete the empty outlines. After class, he asks students to leave their completed outlines along with an exit ticket explaining something they learned and something they are curious about. He is surprised at how insightful his students are in their explanations and also identifies some misunderstandings.

After a discussion on strategies for engagement Mr. Delitto agrees to have students look up and work together to complete a Who, When, Where, and Why chart of the Crusades. He then sets up study teams (he's not sure about using grouping, but decides to purposefully group by ability this time) with each group selecting a different topic from a list: Notable people; economic, religious and other causes; timeline of significant events; map/ geography of the Crusades; outcomes of the Crusades.

Each group develops a contract for the work they plan to do, a task list for each of the members of the team, and a schedule. During their research, Mr. Delitto guides them in planning how they will present their findings to the class. He requires that they provide a note-taking document and that they include review questions at the conclusion of their presentation.

Mrs. Terry visits the class again when the students are presenting their work. Afterwards, the teachers discuss what was successful, and what needs to be changed. Mr. Delitto is satisfied with the students' engagement while at the same time he has some uneasiness with his lack of control over what the class is learning. He recognizes the value of formative assessments embedded in projects and realizes the importance of structuring the assignment and monitoring learning carefully and agrees to try this process again, next time strengthening his students' questioning skills and using strategies such as "Split Judgment" where students record a claim or fact on the left side and evidence that supports (or refutes it) on the right. He also read about and wants to try "nutshelling" for intermittant review and also an ABC summary.

He works on these skills, and is very pleased at his next teacher evaluation when the principal compliments him on his increased engagement of learners, their understanding of the Crusades, and his use of formative assessments to monitor learning.

Emphasis on Growth and Improvement

Growth means that something is developing and progressing over time. It is easy to measure the growth of a child's height or weight but harder to measure their understanding and ability to apply learning. If everyone had the same ideas about growth, policy, practice, and measurement, it would be easy to manage, but we have work to do before that happens.

According to Katherine Castellano and Andrew Ho (2013), a growth model "is a collection of calculations that summarize student performance over two or more time points." This sounds reasonable until you begin to interpret data on value added, gain, scores, or growth percentiles. All of these strategies require complex data analysis. None of them tell you how a child is doing in mastering specific classroom learning targets.

Learning for Mastery

When Benjamin Bloom coined the phrase "learning for mastery" in 1968 he intended it to mean that with just-right conditions, learners would grow towards proficiency. Rebranded *Mastery Learning* in 1971, it continued to emphasize the learning process rather than instructional strategies, or testing methods. Bloom's original intent was to build mastery through feedback and corrective measures. Over time, this has morphed into demonstrations of achievement of standards, often through rigorous accountability measures such as standardized tests.

Backtracking to Bloom's original intent, it becomes clear that assessment is at the heart of true mastery. Assessment provides the evidence of learning, but, more importantly, it is the teacher's response and guidance that supports student mastery. This is similar to health care professionals who receive feedback and monitoring as they demonstrate proficiency on multiple skills. Their certification is not based solely on one standardized test score. In the classroom this idea is supported through a comprehensive range of assessments from fine-grained minute by minute actions, to alternative measures of authentic work, as well as, traditional tests.

There is a gap in education between what research reveals about learning and what standardized tests require and report.

Edward Deci (reported in Dweck, 2008) found carrots and sticks only motivate in the short term. Carol Dweck (2008) builds on his work to explain that learning which is related to a growth mindset and that is built on steps towards personal mastery is optimal to success. This is especially relevant in today's classrooms where diverse learners construct complex understanding through multiple pathways. Daniel Pink (2011) synthesized a range of research to explain that motivation comes from autonomy, mastery, and purpose.

It is when scores and grades are primarily used for rewards and punishments that students and teachers seek short-term rewards rather than long-term intrinsic benefits. These short-term incentives undermine mastery. When mastery, based on engagement and relevance, is placed at the forefront of learning, students then develop a sense of competence that nurtures their motivation to put their best effort into mastering challenging work.

Assessment that is Growth Oriented

Assessment is goal and growth oriented when students improve their knowledge and skills, and develop mastery of explicit standards. Assessment is a means to an end. It is not an end in itself, but rather a step on the path to improvement.

There are numerous formulae and multiple ways to look at growth but none of them are straightforward and easy enough for us to adopt wholeheartedly at the classroom level. In addition, there are many questions to be answered before determining how to assess growth. Is it based on a conglomerate of actions or one final measure? Should colleges make student selection decisions based on SAT scores or high school grades and activities? Would you rather have a wedding dinner prepared by the person who won the TV reality show competition or the one who graduated with top grades from a respected culinary school? Truly, there is not one answer to these questions.

In relation to learning, growth means "the amount of a student's academic progress between two points in time" (Center for Public Education, 2007, p. 1). Their article explains the difference between growth, proficiency, and value added models. So, who would you select to pack your parachute? The student who always scored 92% on parachute packing or the one who started out at 60% and ended up at 100% accuracy (with an average of 80%) in packing a parachute? Once again, there is not an easy answer to measuring improvement or even final scores.

One way to measure growth is by starting with a pretest for a lesson, unit, or year, then compare the scores to an equivalent post-test. As part of an action research project for her graduate class, one teacher willingly took on a class of students with a history of low grades and poor performance on standardized tests. She did this in part to challenge the misconception that a final score is more important than growth measures. She also found deep meaning and gratification in teaching more challenging learners and seeing their excitement as they understood a new idea. Along with three other content area teachers, they designed and administered a pretest that reflected similar knowledge and skills measured by the post-test.

She worked with the other teachers to establish student learning goals for the class with the aim of developing 78 percent proficiency in the students' final score. On the pretest, her class's scores were dismal, with an average of 32 percent. The other classes scored higher, ranging from 48 to 60% proficiency.

Throughout teaching and learning, she used the best practices she knew for classroom management, motivating students, engaging them, and making learning meaningful. She used an array of instructional strategies from teacher delivered to purposeful group work and hands-on projects. She embedded assessments that were relevant, reciprocal, and informative.

At the end of the class her students once again, had the lowest scores. However they rose from an average of 32 percent proficient to 55 percent proficient. She was devastated and feared being labeled a low performing teacher. That was until she decided to use a different calculation that showed her class had a 71% improvement in test outcome. The other classes raised their scores to anywhere between 55% and 78% proficiency reflecting an average 18 percent improvement.

When she arrived for her summative evaluation armed with this data, her administrator was alarmed at the class's low scores, but when the growth data was presented, he changed his thinking and praised the teacher for her success and initiative in recognizing the value of growth measures. To her relief she was not identified as a low performing teacher and is still teaching some of the most remarkable students in her school.

The cognitive sciences explain that progress is not linear. When learning a new language or sport the early pattern is of rapid growth, but over time the visibility of improvement slows down. Sometimes learning feels more like a steep stairway. When you struggle to understand a complex math concept, other solutions become more evident. Sometimes growth means giving up a beloved tool, such as an out of date putter, in favor of a tool that will help you move forward more quickly. It could be a new technology, ingredient, or game strategy when that "aha!" moment clicks.

In Practice

In Ms. Watson's fifth grade class, students are working on projects about branches of governments. She begins by pre-assessing incoming knowledge about government with a display of student responses on *Padlet* (another useful classroom app) where each branch is noted and students post what they know about it. Answers are discussed and lingering questions are quickly sought on personal devices.

Knowledge is constructed on the interactive white board and students complete their own box charts (facts, meaning, connections) for submission and informative feedback. Students then break into groups to research, add details to incoming knowledge, and present their findings (PPT, *Prezi*, *Glogster*, etc.) on the role and power of one branch of government: executive, legislative, or judicial. Colored cups are available to students to signal their progress or need for help, during learning. An exit slip such as a bump in the road or a 3–2–1 (Greenstein, 2010) is routinely used. Students submit their own summary for an interim assessment, get feedback targeted to their content knowledge and organization of information, and develop recommendations for next steps in learning.

After Ms. Watson is satisfied that each student has reached the requisite mastery levels they form groups to create games to be played by others (i.e., *Millionaire*, *Jeopardy*). Assessment criteria are displayed (i.e., accuracy and depth of content, organization, playability, design, creativity, and collaboration). When the games are completed, each group circulates and plays other groups' games. When done, they complete a rubric and leave feedback. Each student also submits their individual game questions and a self-assessment.

Through this balance of pre-, interim-, and post-assessment with individual and collaborative learning, Ms. Watson gives her students autonomy in learning. Monitoring progress towards mastery is done purposefully. A common summative assessment is used by all the fifth grade teachers and she is pleased when her students consistently receive high scores on their understanding of branches of government.

To get the most out of growth models consider the following questions:

1. What is the purpose in collecting the data—is it truly for growth or more for accountability?
2. Who will be most affected by the scores—students, teachers, the community?
3. Who should be held accountable for scores?
4. How should we interpret and respond to the data?
5. What other assessment strategies are suited to our purposes?
6. How can we expand our assessment practices to be sure they are valid, reliable, fair, and balanced?

The Council of Chief State School Officers commissioned a large-scale study of growth models (Castellano and Ho, 2013) with the conclusion that statistical models and accountability systems continue to become more complex and cumbersome generating more data than is feasible to sort and analyze.

Here's an example on one state's calculation for determining the teacher's contribution to a student's growth (Figure 2.4).

Figure 2.4 Formula for a Value Added Growth Model

Source: Florida Department of Education

$$y_{ti} = X_i\beta + \sum_{r=1}^{L} y_{t-r,} \, y_{t-r} + \sum_{q=1}^{Q} Z_{qi}\,\theta_q + e_i^{\,*}$$

$$\tilde{\theta}_j = \frac{N_j\sigma_t^2}{N_j(\sigma_s^2+\sigma_t^2)+\sigma_e^2} \cdot \frac{\sum_{i=1}^{N_j} r_{(j)i}}{N_j}$$

$$r_{ti} = y_{ti} - y_{ti}$$

When each teacher and school returns to the real purpose of growth measures by recording each student's improvement over time, the focus is returned to the learner and their growth rather than the standardized test scores as a basis for teacher evaluations. A pragmatic approach to assessment supports a reasonable and rational approach to teaching and learning. When there is symbiosis between learning and assessing, each one supports the other.

Chapter Summary

Key Ideas

1. Assessment has a powerful role in motivation and success.

2. Informative assessment builds on prior learning and supports growth and improvement.

3. Informative assessment must be purposeful in strategy, placement, and purpose.

4. Accurate interpretations and supportive responses to formative assessment strengthen learning outcomes.

5. Assessment is at its best when it is used to inform rather than to rate and sort students.

6. Transparency in assessment serves all constituents with integrity and fairness.

7. Assessing to mastery is not the same as teaching to the test.

8. Mastery is multidimensional, requiring multiple measures of multifaceted skills.

9. Assessment of mastery entails more than one right answer based on inflexible rules and formulas.

10. Feedback on both the learning process and outcomes must be specific, timely, and actionable in guiding students' next steps.

11. Quality of learning is improved through the recognition and correction of mistakes.

12. Interim benchmark assessments designed by commercial test makers cannot supplant daily formative assessments embedded in classroom instruction.

13. Students need opportunities to show what they know. For example on a multiple choice test, leave a space for them to respond: "If you think you know the answer but may have selected the wrong response, explain what you know in relation to the question."

14. It's okay to make mistakes, as long we learn from them.

15. If we know where we are headed and have good directions, we are more apt to arrive at our destination.

Why this Works

At the center of all this research is one underlying idea: "Formative assessment is a constantly occurring process, a verb, a series of events in action, not a single tool or a static noun" (NCTE, 2013, p. 3).

Assessment, as learning, requires a spectrum of strategies used by teacher and students. While the selection of a strategy is important, it is really the response that makes the difference. Assessment works best when the evidence is used to adjust instruction.

Learners are constantly changing. They bring varied strengths to the classroom. If they don't come in one size, assessment shouldn't either. When they are engaged in learning they are also more engaged in assessment, are much more motivated to achieve, and become more effective self-assessors.

Assessment requires a stream of data, rather than a drop in the bucket, to deeply understand student learning. Evidence doesn't mean one score on one test on one day of the year, but instead means ongoing monitoring of learning.

By the time test data is made available, teachers and students may have missed valuable opportunities to close gaps in learning. Trying to undo learning that has taken hold is much more difficult than shaping learning in process.

Rather than waiting for the media to report test scores, informative assessment emphasizes, encourages, and celebrates growth rather than only final scores.

When assessment and instruction are intertwined, it requires an adjustment to the teaching and assessing formula from teach, test, repeat, to a new paradigm of learn, engage, monitor, and respond.

Assessment is more than a look in the rear-view mirror. It means looking ahead to where you want to be.

Reflection and Application

Case Study for a Professional Learning Group

Teacher of the Year

You have been asked to serve on the committee that selects the district's assessor of the year. This is similar to the teacher of the year recognition, but the standards they are attaining relate to their use of best practice in assessment and the most purposeful collection, analysis, and application of data.

Your group has narrowed the decision down to two candidates, with very different approaches to assessment.

Teacher 1

Teacher 1 teaches third grade all content areas. He uses strategic, well-planned assessment strategies that are based on the new "All Children can Achieve" standards. There is also a local curriculum that includes unit assessments. In addition, his teaching partners have decided on specific district benchmark measures. The grade level teachers also share common assessments during teaching and learning.

The assessments are, in general, traditional measures such as selected choice and completion items as the teachers believe these generate the most valid and reliable data. At the conclusion of each segment of teaching and learning, the teachers review the data charts. They identify students who are performing below grade level on assessment of content knowledge. They also identify those who are at the mean, and those who are achieving beyond standard.

They use this data to plan interventions such as additional support on reading fluency, expanded vocabulary, and sequencing ideas. Each year this teacher's group and school perform the highest in the district on the state mandated tests and benchmarks. This teacher received high scores on the assessment section of their annual evaluation. One concern is that when anyone walks by his room the children are sitting, quietly listening to the teacher, and frequently completing skill-building worksheets.

Teacher 2

This teacher works in a school with looping, so she stays with her students for a couple of years. She loves to engage her students in projects. Rather than teaching specific content on ELA, math, social studies, science, and the arts, she takes an interdisciplinary approach. Student learning aligns with the standards and the grade level curriculum and content. She also uses the district designed measures. Her pre- and post-assessments include core content. They also extend to analysis of varied perspectives, drawing inferences, making connections between ideas, and solving problems.

When she began to use project-based learning a few years earlier, there was evidence of disorder in her room. Students had varied levels of engagement, the purpose of their actions wasn't readily visible, and resources were inconsistently used.

She took two steps to enhance her own skills. She took an online MOOC on project-based learning and this past year, she began to use computer-based projects. Working in small groups, students select a subtopic of the curriculum unit. They also identify what is important to learn about the topic and plan a strategy for their learning. This step is recorded by the students, reviewed by the teacher, and feedback is also provided by peers who also use the process to reciprocally plan their work.

While there were some commonalities among the group's requirements in that each has to identify essential vocabulary, recognize differences and similarities in the resources, synthesize their ideas, and publish their learning outcomes, each takes a different approach. One group designs a *Prezi* on local landforms, another produces a *PowToon* on the weather patterns, a third creates a video mash-up of local waterways, and the last writes a guide on local weather patterns that would be put in a time capsule, along with current artifacts to inform people living in the future.

As each group presents, the class takes structured notes, asks questions, and provides feedback. Students write questions for the unit test (based on the unit objectives) and quiz each other. The teacher incorporates the students' questions into the common grade-level post-test. Concern is expressed about how she differentiates for varied abilities and also about how she responds to evidence of growth towards the standards.

Questions for Reflection

1. What types of evidence should be used in evaluating the candidates?

2. How would you compare qualitative to quantitative student data when making a decision?

3. Identify the top three criteria you would use to select the front-runner.

4. How should the selection be explained to the faculty so that the decision is perceived as a valid one?

3

Sticky Assessment

Objectives of this chapter

1. Realize the motivational value of assessment.
2. Empower and engage students as assessors.
3. Plan assessments that incorporate flexibility and differentiation.
4. Embed assessments throughout teaching and learning.

Where Learning Takes Hold

Sticky: Tending or designed to stick to things on contact (Oxford Dictionaries)

Assessments that are sticky work in two ways. They catch a student's attention, serving as the glue of learning. They also reveal how well the learning is sticking and how deeply the student is learning. Basically, they build and make visible the expanding dendrites and connections that are being constructed in the brain as learning takes place.

Assessments are the bonding agents of learning. They are the traction that cause learning to slow down and take hold. As teachers routinely check-in on students' progress, evidence guides the next steps in both teaching and learning. In this way, measures of knowing become evaluations of understanding that in turn lead to assessments of higher and deeper thinking and complex applications of learning. For example, first graders are showing what they know about time using manipulatives; third graders are planning travel schedules based on their knowledge of time zones; and secondary students are advocating for a later start to the school day. Each with specific assessments aligned to the learning targets.

Sticky assessments are designed around three key concepts.

◆ First, assessment engages and empowers learners. It asks them to consider their learning in relation to the learning targets and criteria. It makes little sense to teach someone how to ice skate by only watching videos of professionals. The learners need to know what is expected on their first day on the ice, what skills they will be building over time, the progress they are making, and strategies for improvement.

◆ Second, assessment is flexible. If students are mastering content vocabulary and are expected to apply it in their writing, the assessments must be flexible and differentiated. The first time anyone visits a foreign country, they may have learned a few essential terms such as zahod, banho, or toilette but may not be able to give or to understand complex direction to its location. Scaffolds and supports are required for the ongoing growth and continuing success of each student.

◆ Third, assessment takes place throughout teaching and learning. We talked about the purpose and placement of assessment in Chapter 2. Equally as important is the idea that routine assessments engage, inform and guide and thus facilitate learning that lasts. Embedded assessments support a spectrum of learning outcomes. They ask the learner to think at increasingly sophisticated levels, make connections beyond themselves, and question deeply.

Assessment that Motivates

Many of the ideas in this chapter are grounded in research from the cognitive sciences. Think for a moment about what motivates you to learn something new. Perhaps it is by necessity, such as when your tire goes flat and you are miles from help. Or maybe it is looking up the historical landmarks or ball parks that interest you in a city that you will be visiting. Motivation is highest when there is something relevant and meaningful to learn or do. It is at these times that the boundaries blur between earning a grade and personal discovery. This is an important place to seek out in the classroom. This is the place where learning occurs because students are actively involved in the experience. Mihaly Csikszentmihalyi (2008) calls this "flow."

Mindset

In addition to being engrossed in learning, a belief that you are a capable learner and can master new tasks is an important motivator. This belief drives us to practice and probe in order to get better. Carol Dweck (2008) refers to this as "mindset." She explains that people with a fixed mindset believe that they are either smart or not and there is nothing they can do about it. Over the years I have heard so many students say "I'm just not good at math." For those students the natural response is to avoid those tasks they find difficult.

In contrast, people with a growth mindset believe they have the capacity to learn and that it is worth the effort to try. They understand that, with practice and determination, they can develop their skills and improve learning outcomes. Dweck discovered that people have more capacity for learning than previously believed and that experience, perseverance, and effort can take us farther than a fixed mindset.

Small changes in the way a teacher responds can support learners in developing a growth mindset. Rather than saying "good job" or "you are so good in writing"; try saying "you worked hard at improving the organization of your project" or "rewriting that sentence made your idea clearer." In refocusing thinking to a growth context, the idea of assessment also must change from measurement of short-term learning to the potential for long-term gain.

Drive

Dan Pink (2011) explains the importance of autonomy, mastery, and purpose in his book *Drive*. He shows how the carrot and stick approach to teaching and testing is unproductive in relation to long-term gains. Self-direction and autonomy are the foundation of independent learning. Purpose is essential to making learning meaningful, but this doesn't mean that fixed teacher-generated goals are the only pathway to learning. When a teacher serves as a mentor, she sets the stage for success while letting each student process learning in their own way.

Pink also describes mastery as a basic human need in that we all want to learn and achieve. This drive is squelched in classrooms where everything is tightly controlled. Directed learning may have worked in 20th-century schools, but 21st-century learners must also be effective problem solvers who can generate innovative ideas.

Purposeful learning is another cornerstone of drive. When learners find meaning and relevance in their work, they are more apt to be engaged and motivated. I recall one student explaining why she didn't answer the writing part of the standardized test. She explained that she had never played in an urban playground and had no interest in the process for planning one so how could she write an essay on the topic. Perhaps scale models and design tools would have provided meaningful autonomy and purpose for her.

Stress Management

Failure is not motivational but many of our most inspirational heroes have faced it. Michael Jordan didn't make the high school basketball team on his first try, Oprah Winfrey overcame tremendous odds, and Walt Disney was told he had no imagination. Learning to pick yourself up again and again, learning from your mistakes, and believing you can do better next time is what drives learners to overcome failure.

Stress has a physiological impact on learning. Researchers in Taiwan used blood samples from middle school students who had just taken a very difficult high-stakes test. The researchers were looking for students who had various versions of the COMT gene. David Goldman (2010), chief of neurogenetics at the National Institutes of Health, calls it the worrier-warrior gene. The COMT gene (Catechol-O-Methyl-Transferase) produces a protein used in brain functioning that inhibits dopamine. Dopamine is a neurotransmitter that regulates emotional responses.

The Taiwan researchers, as explained in a PBS Newshour report (2013), were searching for the gene that either builds or clears dopamine from the frontal cortex. Once they determined the students' genotypes they matched it with test scores. People with the MET version have a slow but steady release of an enzyme that clears dopamine slowly. The result is a more consistent ability to engage in complex thinking helping these people think through challenging problems and foresee outcomes of actions and decisions. But it also results in ongoing levels of anxiety. Under stress, the prefrontal cortex is flooded with dopamine, but is not as efficient at removing it, bogging down thinking in a dopamine wash. The result can be long-term test anxiety.

In the VAL version, at times of stress, the enzyme rapidly streams dopamine into the prefrontal cortex providing an immediate edge to clear thinking. These warriors are ready to fight on short notice. The dopamine quickly rises and almost as quickly gets cleared away. These are the risk takers who like the thrill of just-in-time behavior rather than planning ahead. They tackle a test with confidence and then move on to the next exciting task. They face failure as a challenge to overcome.

Neither type is better than the other, but test takers with high levels of test anxiety may not fare as well as those who receive a quick hit of dopamine. But of course, as with any behavior, the complexity of human beings makes this another point of interest to keep in mind in the testing room. Judy Willis (2014a), explains more about the science behind stress and our responses to it. She reports that acute stress inhibits learning. This underscores the importance of a positive classroom environment that provides the support and scaffolds that each child needs.

A few recommended strategies for helping students reduce stress include:

- recognize and utilize those strategies and routines that improve your personal success;
- develop a system for managing assignments and deadlines;
- take a deep breath and work at a pace and depth that feels comfortable;
- believe in the value of mindset and drive in supporting your success; and
- scrutinize learning outcomes, identify areas for growth, seek extra help.

Relationship Building

"At the heart of every school community is one very important word: relationships. Relationships are what support and guide students to achieving goals, they are what build empathy, and they are what tie communities together" (Clara Galan, 2015).

Success is often built on relationships with those around us. We have each had a mentor, friend, or family member who provided that safe harbor combined with robust inspiration and a strong belief in our abilities. For students, this starts with a capable, caring, and responsive teacher. Just as in baking, certain skills and knowledge are essential, but it was grandma's special dose of love that always made her chocolate chip cookies the best. She probably told you that it took her years of fine-tuning and tasting the cookies that really made them perfect. And she did this just for you. It was this personalization and differentiation that made them delicious. Of course, she also never told you that she made them with butterscotch chips for your cousin.

In the classroom, a sense of community is essential to achievement. Students who feel encouraged and supported are more willing to learn new skills, consider different ideas, and learn from mistakes. The teacher's respect and compassion becomes reciprocal. Building rapport is worth the attention it takes in creating a respectful and collaborative classroom.

Checkpoint on Motivation

While there are many ideas on motivation, there is no magic bullet that works for every student on every assignment. For now reflect on your own experiences with motivation.

1. What motivates you; what gets you excited to learn more about something? Think about the things that make you want to continue to learn and feel satisfied and gratified.
2. Think about a time that you weren't especially motivated to complete a required task. What blocked your motivation? How did you feel, what did you do to overcome the obstacles?
3. Think about a student who you have difficulty motivating. What steps will you take to plan, teach, and assess in ways that encourage a growth mindset, foster drive, reduce stress, and build relationships?

Students as Assessors

There are contradictory ideas about brains at rest. Neuroscientists believe that when the brain is resting (a.k.a., not being asked to perform a specific action), it is taking the opportunity to strengthen memories and embed learning. Alternatively, a mind that is not used and has nothing to remember becomes bored and disengaged. However, there is a difference between the brain at rest and the brain when it lacks stimulation. Finding the balance between over stimulating the brain and boredom is an important component of sticky assessment. When learning any new skills, mastery is built step by step. Similar to skiing, having just come off the bunny slope, most sensible people would assess their outcome and head for the next level rather than the double black diamond.

Assessment Habits

"Quality is not an act, it is a habit": Aristotle.

What does it take to develop and engage the mind and strengthen the relationship between learning and assessing? Habits such as regular exercise are beneficial to health which is supported by a balanced diet. There are also mental habits that support learning which in turn contribute to success.

Experts on habits praise their value. Stephen Covey's (1989) first habit is to "Be Proactive," and his second is to "Begin with the End in Mind." In relation to learning and assessing he is asking us to think about where we are headed and what steps we can take to get there.

Art Costa and Bena Kallick (2009) describe "habits of mind" as a fundamental set of behaviors that support thoughtful teaching and learning. From their list of 16, 6 are especially pertinent to assessment.

1. *Persisting*: Sticking with something and seeing it to completion. Looking for ways to reach your goals. Not giving up.

2. *Striving for Accuracy*: Maintaining high standards. Always doing your best and seeking to produce quality work.

3. *Remaining Open to Continuous Learning*: Recognizing that there is much more to know. Making every effort to stretch your learning.

4. *Thinking Flexibly*: Looking at a situation from multiple perspectives in order to understand its complexity. Recognizing that there may be alternative ways to solve a problem.

5. *Taking Responsible Risks*: Seeking a safe environment where weaknesses may be recognized while at the same time using this awareness for improvement.

6. *Thinking about Thinking* (Metacognition): The ability to stand back and consider our thoughts and actions in relation to the goal. Recognizing what we know and what we don't know and strategizing next steps.

Matthew Egbert and Xabier Barandiaran (2014) describe habits as patterns of behavior that are supported by secure structures and built through successful repetition. They rely on the work of Edward Thorndike (1911) who explained that a response to a situation will become stronger the more it is connected with that situation. This goes beyond a simple stimulus-response reaction in that the habits become part of the self-monitoring foundations of learning.

Extending and connecting these ideas to education means that well-developed and productive habits are the underpinnings of successful teaching, learning, and assessing. These habits help students learn and guide teachers in gathering informative and accurate insights about student achievement. In turn, the assessment results are used to support ongoing growth and improve learning outcomes.

Checkpoint on Habits

Check the correct answer.

Continuously working at finishing a task:

1. Flexibility _____ 2. Precision _____ 3. Persistence _____

Reflecting on one's own thoughts and actions:

1. Metacognition _____ 2. Creativity _____ 3. Openness _____

Thinking about new ways to solve a problem:

1. Questioning _____ 2. Flexibility _____ 3. Risk Taking _____

Answers: 3, 1, 2

Which habits do you consider most important?

What habits do you consistently use to support your success?

What habits do you want to develop?

- In yourself:
- In your students:

Engaging Learners

Going beyond one's comfort zone seems less risky when a safety net is in place. In the classroom this may include modified learning goals or additional time for mastery. A teacher can sequence assessments such that the questions become more difficult as the student proceeds. A student can decide at what point the test is too much of a stretch beyond the comfort zone and will result in pointless frustration rather than an accurate assessment of learning.

There are many voices advocating for student-centered assessment, but what does that really mean and what types of assessment involve and motivate learners? These ideas are based on the work of Heidi Andrade, Kristen Huff, and Georgia Brooke (2012); James McMillan (2011); National Research Council (2001); and Amy Woytek (2007). Following this list you will find detailed explanations of selected strategies.

For Learners

- ◆ Facilitate students as goal setters and planners;
- ◆ encourage students as record keepers and self-monitors;
- ◆ empower student choice in achieving and assessing goals;
- ◆ incorporate self-assessment based on clearly defined learning outcomes and indicators of learning; and
- ◆ boost students' metacognitive/reflective skills.

By Teachers

- ◆ Appreciate that learning is supported by engagement with real-world problems;
- ◆ offer reasonable challenge with purposeful scaffolds;
- ◆ emphasize growth and improvement, not solely final grades;
- ◆ routinely monitor and respond to progress and gaps in student learning;
- ◆ Provide targeted, specific, and actionable feedback; and
- ◆ use information from ongoing monitoring to advise teaching and learning.

The elements of self-assessment are best viewed as a cyclical, ongoing process as shown in Figure 3.1 where students identify the targets they are aiming for, monitor progress during learning, and self-evaluate outcomes. This informs the learner of where and when they need to modify the learning targets or alter their path through them.

Figure 3.1 The Cyclical Process of Self-Assessment

A visitor to a highly motivational classroom will see students actively engaged in planning and choosing learning pathways, selecting resources, working towards targeted learning outcomes, and monitoring progress. Mr. Richards' room is not a quiet place, but it is obvious that noise is purposeful. One group is making a video on overcoming barriers to healthy eating, another on cross-cultural eating patterns, and a third is comparing and analyzing research on nutrition. The overarching class goal is to develop persuasive fact-based statements that encourage healthy eating.

Students plan their own short-term goals, monitor their learning with progress logs, and present their work to the class (and sometimes a larger audience) along with assessments that they have designed to check their audience's understanding of their presentation. Their final analysis of the concepts of healthy eating is kept in a portfolio such as a *LiveBinders* where they record and monitor learning, maintain resources, and compile various types of assessments that gauge their progress and achievement. Mr. Richards sees his role as a facilitator, questioner, guide to resources, and continuous prod and nudge to higher and deeper learning.

Choice Boosts Accountability

When learners have choice, they develop a sense of empowerment. When we give children a choice of dinner vegetable they are more apt to eat it. In an engaging classroom students are routinely given choices. They are all required to work towards a common learning target and complete assignments but can select the learning strategy (visually explain a concept, graphically organize learning, make an instructional video) and assessments. The underlying idea is that providing choice gives students control over their learning. One easy way do this is to add an H to a KWL symbolizing *How* will I know what I have learned.

Project- and choice-based learning is best supported with clear guidelines, routine teacher and self-monitoring, and technically sound assessment. A meta-analysis by Ericka Patall, Harris Cooper, and Jorgianne Robinson (2008) found a strong link between choice and motivation. At the same time, they caution that too much choice can have a diminishing return when students are unclear about the path and expected outcomes of learning.

With choice comes increased accountability. As students set their own learning targets and formulate their own learning plans, they are also developing a sense of ownership and responsibility for their achievement. At the conclusion of their work they have varied opportunities to show what they have learned. Their options vary with the level of complexity or depth required. For example an assessment of knowing and understanding may require labeling a diagram. An application of learning may ask students to make a change at the checkout. Higher level thinking involves comparing and contrasting two authors' ideas, and finally synthesizing ideas into a new solution or product.

Their purposeful choice of showing what they know must align with the intentional learning targets. A choice board, as shown in Table 3.1, can support differentiation.

Table 3.1 Assessment Choice Board

Level of Learning	Choice 1	Choice 2	Choice 3
Recall and understand	Arrange puzzle pieces of the story into the correct sequence	Illustrate/write the 3 steps	Write questions to use in a peer review of new vocabulary
Scrutinize, analyze, and apply	Develop and add a new character. Explain his purpose and influence on the storyline	Defend how your notes and resources align with the learning targets	Explore experts' solutions to a problem: Design a pros/cons graphic
Synthesize and create	Sell your story to a book publisher	Design a game to help others review their learning	Develop and defend an original solution to a problem

Encouraging Metacognition

"In the current era of standards-based education, student self-assessment stands alone in its promise of improved student motivation, engagement, and learning" (McMillan and Hearn, 2008, p. 40). This does not mean that students simply check-off their achievements, but rather use multifaceted strategies to assess their learning.

As assessors, students continuously evaluate their learning against the goals they set out to learn. This information is then used to guide their ongoing actions. It determines whether they stay on the current path, seek new resources, ask additional questions, or take a step back to reconsider and refine their plans and goals. It is this ongoing metacognitive process that moves them towards the goals.

When students are curators of their learning, using evidence to support learning, monitoring progress, and reflecting on these elements, they are more apt to be engaged and motivated. An important component of self-assessment is metacognition. Scott Paris and Alison Paris (2001) explain that "self-assessments include cognitive, motivational, and affective factors . . . that require the internalization of standards so students can regulate their own learning more effectively" (p. 95).

John Hattie (2009) found metacognition to have a powerful effect size of .69. Assessment strategies for supporting this high-yield approach include:

1. explaining connections to prior learning, previous readings, settings, and activities;
2. justifying self-directed decisions about learning;
3. making choices in displaying learning;
4. using annotated rubrics to assess real-world problem solving (Hattie (2011) ranks the teaching of problem solving at .61 effect); and
5. self-analysis of scores.

Hattie has put self-reporting of grades at the top of his list, but his research shows that this varies with students' cognitive ability.

Table 3.2 shows a metacognition that students can use when assessments and tests are returned and reviewed. The student can identify the influences on their scores. The teacher then uses this to identify common concerns such as needing more background knowledge or checking that questions are clearly written. This summative strategy also gives students an opportunity to elaborate on their misunderstandings, their need for more directed instruction, or problems within the assessments.

Table 3.2 Student Self-Assessment

Assignment, or question number	Made a simple mistake	Need more study, time, or practice	Didn't understand the question/ assignment	Need more teacher-guided instruction	This is way too hard for me (because)	Comments, elaboration, my next steps

In Practice: Motivational Assesment

Ms. Wallen combines choice, goal setting, self-monitoring, and self-assessment in her unit on the seasons. Previous to my visiting her class I watched a group of Southern California first graders sort icons of the seasons into summer, fall, winter, and spring. A few got stuck on the image of sledding having never seen snow or sleds. In this aha! moment I was reminded that students bring their own experiences to learning and these can include misconceptions. As shown in an often shared YouTube video, the majority of Harvard graduates do not have a clear understanding of the seasons as many explain that the earth's orbit is an ellipse thus, when it is closer to the sun, the weather is warmer.

Using this awareness, Ms. Wallen begins the unit by activating prior knowledge and having students frame questions about the seasons (earlier in the year she built questioning skills in her students to support purposeful inquiry sequences throughout the taxonomy). Some questions they ask are:

◆ Why do the seasons change?
◆ Why are seasons different in different places?
◆ How fast does the earth orbit around the sun?
◆ What if the earth didn't tilt, spin, or orbit?

The large-scale goals for the unit are the same for everyone:

◆ cite textual evidence;
◆ integrate content presented in diverse formats; and
◆ explain how the relationship between the tilt of the Earth's axis and its annual orbit around the sun results in seasons.

Each group determines their own local goals and process:

◆ One wants to understand the earth's rotations better, another is curious about the tilt of the axis, and a third wants to compare sunrise/sunset schedules to the seasonal rotations in different points of the world.

The learning strategies are unique for each small group:

- One develops a model of the earth's rotation, another uses flashlights and fruit to demonstrate seasons, a third creates an e-book using *Zooburst*, and another produces a video with *imovie* or *animoto*.

The assessments are consistent for all the students:

- a learning log of initial questions and planned learning strategies;
- an ongoing log of learning process and outcomes;
- a rubric for their presentations (accuracy, clarity, data-based, logical sequence, fits time frame, includes student assessment);
- a quick quiz on content knowledge: for example: Where on the earth do the seasons change the least? Explain what seasons are illustrated in these pictures, define axis, hemisphere, poles;
- explain it to a Martian—structured writing assignment; and
- metacognition: I used to think, but now I know, because . . .

Checkpoint on Engagement, Choice, and Megacognition

Consider ways you will use these ideas in your setting.

1. With your professional learning community, think, pair, and share on your beliefs about the value of engagement. Give yourself a 1 if it is unimportant up to a 5 if you believe it is of great significance in making learning stick.
2. How will you provide choice while maintaining consistent standards?
3. What strategies will you use to support students in monitoring and self-assessing their learning?

4. How will you respond to gaps and misunderstandings that are revealed as students develop their self-assessment skills?

Reasonable Challenge

Finding that fine balance between pushing students beyond what they can accomplish and letting them travel down a path that is too easy requires precision and sensitivity. Like the caveat "trust but verify" the adage here is "challenge but safeguard."

This begins by substantiating that the level of challenge is reasonable for students. It may take some time to assess their incoming skills and knowledge but it is well worth doing so before placing the diving board over water that is too deep.

Pre-assessments can be done at the start of the school year, at the beginning of a unit, or as part of daily routines. Strategies include quick quizzes that assess mastery of previous learning, or linkages where students connect, predict, and question what they have and are going to learn. Alternatively, students can sticky-post answers to math problems or display what they recall of groups of the periodic table. This information guides the design of a structured sequence of learning that is challenging, achievable, and engaging.

For students who need support learning targets are attuned a sequenced challenge means starting out by asking a student who is learning content vocabulary to use that vocabulary in a paragraph. Their next step is to summarize learning using that vocabulary in writing or graphic display. Once they have mastered the vocab basics, comparing and contrasting can stretch them to the next level of evaluating the logic of an argument, and finally they can synthesize it into a personal perspective and use it to solve real-world problems. Like learning to do puzzles, after the 12-piece before working toward the thousand piece.

As incoming skills and knowledge are validated, instruction can be adjusted accordingly. This may necessitate differentiating content, adjusting pacing, selecting alternative resources, and grouping purposefully. Monitoring for understanding with learning trackers can verify student growth, identify misunderstandings, and inform interventions. Probing for understanding means asking why they believe as they do or how they came up with their answer. Along the way build curiosity and connections to boost reasonable challenge.

When you ask students to rise to a new challenge be sure supports and scaffolds are available. When used sequentially, the expectations remain high for all students as they are monitoring growth towards higher and deeper levels.

In Practice: Students as Assessors

Students in Mr. Jackson's class are excited about an upcoming unit on digital literacy. As early teens, they are avid social networkers who use their devices habitually. He is planning this unit on the writing standard that requires students to write arguments to support claims with clear reasons and relevant evidence, organize ideas logically, and cite credible sources.

He begins by asking the students to identify current concerns and controversies in technology, as they relate to schools. Their brainstorming is posted on a *Padlet* where students also rate the importance of each topic. Ideas include tweeting for learning, risks of snap-chat, cyber-bullying, flipped classrooms, and Internet privacy. Small groups gather around topics of interest to them and begin to brainstorm what they know, what questions they have, how they will learn more, and how their work will be assessed.

The class uses *Google Docs* to post and track their work, receive feedback from other groups, self-monitor learning through checklists and progress logs. Mr. Jackson uses a tightly structured project process that begins with a progression of standards and learning outcomes through levels of the taxonomy. Students are required to specify their groups' learning targets, select resources, monitor learning, synthesize ideas, and determine a strategy for combining individual student research, work, and ideas, into a collective product and presentation.

During the project, students maintain a daily learning log, receive feedback from peers and teacher with insightful questioning, and guidance on next steps. They are also required to write test questions on their presentations. Presentations are peer-scored using a structured rubric that includes depth of research, organization and clarity of presentation, and use of facts and evidence to support their ideas, analysis, and recommendations.

Flexible Assessment

There is no shortage of evidence that human beings are each unique. Based on our talents, personalities, and preferences, we each have our own way of looking at the world and interacting with it. In turn, teaching, learning, and assessing needs to be responsive to the uniqueness of each learner. In the classroom a teacher may find Amadan with his nose in a book about plants while Suzu is gathering and organizing a group to work on designing and planting an organic community garden. So, how do you go about assessing each of them?

Differentiation

From research on learning styles to brain wiring it is generally accepted that although our brains have much in common it is the differences that make each of us unique. We vary in food preferences, clothing styles, choice of media, and more. Yet, in the classroom, there are standardized learning outcomes and curricula that teachers are required to teach and students are expected to master. The framers of the Common Core Standards believed that common standards would "ensure that all students have the skills and knowledge necessary to succeed in college, career, and life upon graduation from high school" (p. 1).

Few educators today embrace the regulated ideas of Thorndike and Skinner as the best way to prepare learners for our complex knowledge-based world. The old factory model of education is no longer relevant. At the same time, teachers worry that they are not able to address everyone's individual needs throughout teaching and learning. In this section you will find concepts and strategies that support differentiation while teaching and assessing a coherent curriculum. While it is not possible to provide 20+ personalized lessons on Edgar Allen Poe, it is possible to offer assessments that are equitable and developmentally appropriate.

Carol Tomlinson (www.caroltomlinson.com) has been a consistent leader and advocate for the value and use of differentiated instruction for nearly two decades. Her work has informed much of our practice in differentiation. She explains that differentiating means recognizing and responding to the variations among learners by giving them multiple options for taking in information and showing their learning.

Glossary of Education Reform says that "differentiation refers to a wide variety of teaching techniques and lesson adaptations that educators use to instruct a diverse group of students, with diverse learning needs, in the same course/classroom."

Differentiation also has a valuable role in assessment. It means starting where the students are, and then building their self-confidence and self-reliance as learners and assessors by providing opportunities for growth and success. Differentiation is the way a teacher anticipates and responds to a variety of students' needs in the classroom through modifications to content, process, and products of assessment. It is not as much about changing the standards but more about adjusting how students can achieve them. Carol Tomlinson and Tonya Moon, explain that "Assessment is the compass for daily planning in a differentiated classroom" (Tomlinson and Moon, 2013, p. 8).

Equity in assessment means there is an imperative to serve all students equally well whether they are English language learners, come from different cultures or ethnic groups, learn in different ways, or bring different strengths to the classroom. Some students are more outspoken while others are more reserved. Some prefer working independently and others in a group; some want the freedom for self-expression and others want to comply with the authority's requirements.

It makes me wonder why it is okay to give one student glasses so they can see the math problem more clearly but not provide a video tutorial for another student who learns better through that modality. When it comes to our differences in digital literacy, physical coordination, or EQ (emotional quotient), we all need adjustments and adaptations to support peak performance. In relation to classroom assessment consider these modifications:

CONTENT: Complexity (breadth, depth), resources
  (written, auditory, visual);

PROCESS: Instructional strategies, chunking learning, timing, grouping; and

PRODUCT: Starting and ending points, ways to show learning, accountability and growth.

Differentiating Content: Moderate the Complexity

One of the first steps in planning instruction is to identify the learning outcomes. Typically there is a range of intended outcomes from content knowledge to understanding and applying, and ultimately to innovating and generating of new ideas. For most students it is best to portion complex outcomes into smaller chunks. Also, begin at lower levels of the taxonomy to support understanding before going on to higher levels of application and analysis.

In Practice: Moderate the Breadth and Depth of Learning

Mr. Gaulin gives Arthur the same unit outline as the rest of the class, but highlighting parts of it helps him focus his learning on specific and clear-cut targets. On the test at the end of the unit, Arthur answers the questions that align with the highlighted part of the unit outline.

Manage the Sources/Amount/Types of Information

Some students learn best by looking at visual materials whether written or dynamic while others prefer auditory channels. Some prefer to seek their own resources but may need guidance on selecting ones relevant to what they are expected to know, understand, and do with their learning. After a teacher-led introduction to maps, independent work on the lesson could include materials such as local paper maps, satellite images, and computer tutorials. For some students, the teacher provides a book on the topic and for others guides an Internet search to find the answers to specific questions. In this way the differentiation is not solely to the content but also to how the student receives it.

In Practice: Regulate the Amount of Vocabulary

For some students, visually seeing too much information on a sheet of paper or a test can be overwhelming. Their pace of reading and responding can be slowed down by too many choices. In science class, Amanda is given the same brief or reading as everyone in the class but her multiple choice questions are reduced from four choices to two.

When only the smallest part of the moon is visible, the moon is said to be in which phase:

A. waning phase   B. new moon phase

Original question: When only a small part of the moon is visible, the moon is in its . . .

Also included C: first quarter, and D: closing stage.

Differentiating Process: Multiple Ways to Learn

Wouldn't it be wonderful if we could all learn to cook the same recipes in the same way? Most readers are probably thinking, no. Some of you would never substitute dried herbs for fresh ones in grandma's roast lamb recipe. When we watch a food show where all the contestants are making meatloaf, do we root for the one who does it like we do or the one who tempts our taste buds with unique flavors? As with cooking, there are many ways for students to learn about topics such as the Crusades or the universe: novels, non-fiction, primary source material, virtual field trip, guest speaker, as well as student production of slide shows, videos, and other e-resource publications on a topic or perspective of their choice. What is more important than the strategy is alignment with the standards.

Embed Formative Assessments

If you arrive in the middle of a ball game you may check with the person next to you to see who is pitching. Learning that Sandy Koufax is pitching a no-hitter is a different scenario from learning that your team is on their third pitcher and still losing. Pre-assessment sets the stage for learning. Teachers can check incoming awareness by probing for background knowledge and identifying connections to prior learning. Monitoring learning during instruction can be done with a cause/effect statement or a graphic displaying of learning and certainly checking on learning after instruction but before the summative can provide insights into lingering gaps.

Chunking Learning and Assessment

Whenever possible, include a summative assessment at the end of each segment of a larger unit. In doing so, students have less to "memorize" before the big test and misunderstandings can be identified early. One teacher I know uses mini (but alternative) versions of the final test throughout teaching and learning. In this way there are no surprises for her or her students on the summative.

Adjust Timing

Assessments can be adjusted to fit the available time by trimming the number and types of questions. Alternatively, students can be given additional time to complete an assessment such as a test or project.

Purposeful Grouping: Independent, Small, or Large Group

For some students, an individually completed graphic organizer is most appropriate and for others, collaboratively designing an infographic using *Piktochart* is best. A teacher may use a mixed group for summarizing learning and homogenous grouping for reading new materials. In this way a teacher can provide scaffolds for some students and rely on peer review for others.

In Practice: Tracking Progress

For some students the use of a daily learning log where they record the learning processes on a short-term basis is the best way to support them. For others, a learning tracker to record progress on specified learning targets works well. Self-assessment is also a form of tracking and can be tightly structured or more metacognitive. For example, Mrs. Ebani gives a learning tracker to his class during a unit on science fiction. All students record key vocabulary. During the unit students read different novels and source material but answer a similar question on the author's main ideas and on distinguishing facts from opinion. During their writing, Wallace uses a checklist to review spelling while Alexandria is asked to reflect on her variety of sentence structures. Throughout learning Mrs. Ebani has frequent check-ins where students are organized in purposeful groups to summarize and share their learning. Before she assigns the summative assignment, she reviews their learning trackers to identify gaps that inform the need for additional support or potential for enrichment.

Differentiating Product: Inform and Illuminate the Products

Along with clear directions on the task and its purpose, students need to know how the outcomes will be assessed. Will they be expected to take a selected choice test (this causes anxiety in many) or will they be encouraged to present and explain their learning (contributes to angst in others), or will they have a choice? If there are expected products such as slides or a video, it is essential to show exemplars. Mr. Zyrl shows products from previous years, provides the scoring rubric, then asks students to score these examples and make recommendations for improvement.

Tiered Outcomes

Based on pre-assessments and targeted content, students' demonstration of learning can be tiered and sequenced like the earth's layers. Everyone starts with the crust, the essential content knowledge while some dig deeply into the inner core. As students master each level they move on to application and analysis of new learning. For example, one student's brochure on animal extinction includes illustrations of animals, another's displays data on the rates, and another's provides persuasive support and strategies for responding to the issue.

This is not much different from computer-adaptive large-scale assessments. As students demonstrate mastery the computer recognizes their strength of understanding and adjusts the subsequent questions to provide reasonable challenge but not overwhelm learners with material they cannot comprehend.

In her classroom, Mrs. Watkins has begun to design her unit assessments in a sequence that aligns with Bloom's taxonomy. She front-loads recall and understanding questions and puts higher level analysis and evaluation later in the test. As she distributes, she subtly marks a stopping point for Marcus, Imenda, and Oliver, typically a little beyond their demonstrated learning but not so far as to frustrate them.

Adjust the Goal Posts

At times, the end point of learning needs to be adjusted. The large-scale standard says that all fourth graders will "Use place value understanding and properties of operations to perform multi-digit arithmetic." And specifically "Multiply a whole number of up to four digits by a one-digit whole number, and multiply two two-digit numbers, using strategies based on place value and the properties of operations. Illustrate and explain the calculation by using equations, rectangular arrays, and/or area models." For some learners this may mean ensuring that they sufficiently demonstrate understanding of place value before moving forward or mastering two-digit multiplication before four-digit.

In Practice: Provide Multiple Ways to Show Learning

Choice is a strategy for engaging students in achieving the learning targets. It supports individual strengths as well as stretching students into unfamiliar territory by allowing them to show learning through multiple modalities such as in writing, visually, with a product, or a performance.

Choice boards generally include alternatives to traditional selected choices and essays. Using them allows students to choose ways to earn points through multiple strategies that are tiered and personalized. The choice board can also be designed to highlight varied levels of Bloom's Taxonomy and Webb's Depth of Knowledge. In the example below students select strategies that add up to 10 points (strategies and points can be adjusted).

Before they begin, their plan is reviewed by the teacher to be sure it is focused on the standards, appropriate to the learning, and stretches them a little past their comfort zone. Kenan chooses

Table 3.3 Multiple Ways to Show Learning

2 Points: Remember	4 Points: Understand, apply	8 Points: Analyze, evaluate, create
Make a word cloud using unit vocabulary	Explain three main ideas from the unit to a Martian	Prepare a technology-based presentation that summarizes the main ideas from the unit
Prepare flash cards that another person can use to review their learning	Use illustrations and words to explain a key concept from the unit	Create a cartoon about the key points of the unit
Construct a picture dictionary of 5 new words from the unit	Write and perform a 30 second public service announcement about your topic that includes 5 words from the unit and an urge to action	Write a mini-test that includes 3 types of questions and measures the 4 targets that were reviewed at the beginning of the unit

to use *HaikuDeck.com* to summarize learning along with flash cards using *Kahoot.it*. Karine decides to explain the main ideas to a Martian and then support that with all three of the 2 point choices. Table 3.3 shows a choice board with multiple ways for students to show learning.

Additional assessable outcomes for choice boards can include a letter of advice, press release, letter to the editor, design of a review game, curation of a *LiveBinder*, graphic organizer, virtual tour, complex questioning, predicted outcomes, prepare a timeline, label an image, explain the difference between, describe different viewpoints, or solve a problem. When using alternative strategies be sure to always check the alignment between learning outcomes, strategies to support it, and assessments that measure it.

Differentiating with Technology

Pokie Stanford, Margie Crowe, and Hollie Flice (2010) explain that "Differentiated instruction with the use of technology offers the opportunity for teachers to engage students in different modalities, while also varying the rate of instruction, complexity levels, and teaching strategies to engage and challenge students" (p. 1).

With *Plickers, Kahoot, Google Forms, Quia,* and *Socrative* teachers can create quizzes, students can post their individual answers, and teachers get immediate information on their learning. Questions can be embedded into a video with *Zaption.* Using this technology, the video can be stopped and understanding can be checked before moving forward.

Students can post a summary of their learning using *Padlet* or *Linoit* and leave digital exit cards on *Google Docs.* They can sort new learning using a graphic organizer such as *Coggle.it* or *bubbl.us.* They can present their learning to others using *PowToon* and a myriad of other presentation tools. QR codes have multiple purposes. You can create a QR code with a QR Generator. When students click on the link they can be taken to personalized videos and visuals or can find the scoring guides for an assignment. It's as easy as taking a picture.

For students who need additional support consider using *Kahn Academy, SchoolTube,* or *WatchKnowLearn.* Purposefully choosing technology for teaching and learning is a way to engage students, make learning stick, and differentiate assessment.

In Practice: Professional Learning Group Case Study on Differentiated Assessment

You have been teaching in an increasingly diverse community and over the past few years students from numerous ethnic and cultural groups have been joining your classroom. You have always included a world-view project in your class but have concerns about doing it this year. It's not the global perspective that concerns you, but rather the process you have used.

In the past, each student selected a country, created a portfolio of its history, geography, folklore, holidays (both religious and social), food patterns, and more. Some years, students worked in small groups to complete projects. There were formative assessments along the way such as learning logs and peer feedback, and summative assessments including a rubric for content, process, product, and presentation. The teachers at the school share a common grade level test on knowledge and understanding of different cultures.

In doing your research in the types of diversity you have discovered some patterns that influence learning. Some girls are taught that their role is to be passive, other students come with a belief that speaking their mind is the norm, some are more oriented toward contributing to the welfare and success of the group without taking personal credit, and others want to be sure everyone knows what they have contributed. There are those who don't want to be told how to complete their project and others who want very specific rules and guidance on its design. You also have three special needs students: One who is non-verbal but highly creative in the production of graphics and illustrations, one with mild Asperger's who has difficulty working with others, and one who is content to let her aide do her work for her.

If you were meeting with other grade level teachers to decide how to teach the unit this year how would you:

1. View the project through the eyes of your students and adjust its design to support differentiation while holding all students accountable for common standards.

2. Consider and incorporate the qualities and strengths of each learner.

3. Differentiate the assessment content, process, and products?

Embedded Assessment

The best learning takes place when frequent check-ins and assessments are part of the process. You may be invited to listen to a 3-hour lecture on quantum mechanics but if you didn't brush up on nanometers, wave-particle duality, the uncertainty principle, and Planck constant you would most likely not learn enough to display your learning beyond the spelling and definitions of some of the terms. But when the presenter stops to check-in on your understanding, you have the opportunity to ask questions and the speaker can identify misconceptions and adjust the material accordingly.

When I talk with secondary social studies teachers they often scratch their heads at students' errors in understanding and recalling prior learning. At the start of a unit on the Opium Wars they discover that some students cannot explain imperialism in 1850. When they begin to discuss the suffrage movement, they find limited awareness of women's rights. When doing map work many are unable to distinguish between longitude and latitude. It's hard to know why this happens, but I have a few conjectures.

Perhaps this is because the curriculum map allows for the study of Greek history in five days, the Age of Enlightenment in four, and the Vietnam War in six. It could be that the common grade level assessments are recall-based rather than asking students to apply learning and solve problems. Or maybe, as teachers, we need to check-in with our students more often. Scripted lessons may be setting an unreasonable time frame and project-based learning is complex in its design and process. It is easy to assign a project with a due date but it takes more purposeful assessment to review the students' proposal for inclusion of clearly stated and aligned learning outcomes, to assess their selection of resources during their work, or for self- or peer assessment before their final submissions so that modifications can be made in order for their final project to align with the learning targets for content, process, and product.

Integrating Learning and Assessing

The concept of assessment that is integrated throughout teaching and learning is built on the research on diagnostic assessment as well as formative assessment. While standardized tests provide information on mastery of specific types of learning, embedded assessments provide opportunities for students to show their current knowledge and skills without having to stop their learning for a formal assessment. What makes embedded assessment different is that students often do not even notice they are being assessed.

A study from BEAR, the Berkeley Evaluation and Assessment Research (Wilson and Sloane, 2000), monitored the implementation of an assessment system that relied on multiple embedded strategies. The assessment of essential concepts and skills was integrated directly into instructional materials rather than given at the conclusion of teaching and learning. Evidence gathered from students who participated in the BEAR model and those who didn't, showed that significant gains can be realized by closer attention to assessment at the classroom level along with a systematic approach to gathering and using assessment information.

In ELA, math, social studies, science, health, and other subjects, knowledge leads to understanding that sticks better if students are involved in manipulating data, synthesizing components, and generating new configurations. In place of the traditional model of teaching and testing, ongoing embedded assessments emphasize growth towards understanding. This could mean checking in on each step of a multiple step math problem or in understanding how shared beliefs influenced the development of civilizations.

An important component of embedded assessment is student ownership. A feasible sequence for building ownership looks like this: Students recognize the learning targets and assess their own starting point.

1. Strategies for achieving the targets are made visible. Students are provided with a selection of ways to approach the targets and are provided with exemplars of the outcomes of learning.
2. Multiple scoring methods that include a balance of formative, alternative, and traditional are explained so that students understood the purpose, weight, and types of assessments.
3. With their teacher, students develop a learning contract/blueprint outlining their goals, strategies, and products/outcomes of learning.
4. Students design a plan for learning and identify their specific steps along the path.
5. Students continuously track and monitor their learning.
6. Ongoing feedback focuses on progress made and strategies for correction.

7. Opportunities for revision and improvement are provided.
8. Summative scoring is based on growth as well as final outcomes.

Assessment as Learning

We all learn from experience. The most memorable or successful learning often takes place at those times where the assessment is the learning. Such as when you are learning to cook and have to quickly distinguish between blanching and boiling the tomatoes. Or when you take time to reflect and analyze the most effective as well as less successful parts of a new unit plan.

Throughout teaching and learning multiple assessment strategies keep students moving forward. At the start of a lesson or unit, they let the teacher know what each student knows and can do. Let's return to Ms. Sindor's class (Chapter 1, p. 25) where she began by posting and discussing the unit objectives. Her students record their scores on the pre-assessment in their learning tracker and make note of their misunderstandings. As the lesson begins, students stand in a circle. Key concepts of digestion are placed in the center of the circle. Each student is given a card with an explanation of one concept. One by one each student places their explanation on a concept. As the activity progresses students may relocate cards as they add their own. At the end, they discuss questions or confusions then record the information on a partially complete graphic organizer that illustrates digestive organs and processes.

Each day of the unit Ms. Sindor has the question of the day posted and then uses a similar but more complex question as an exit slip. The questions become progressively more challenging. For example on the first day she asks where the physical breakdown of food begins and on the exit slip asks which organ pushes food to the stomach by a process calls peristalsis. She collects the slips or has students post their replies to Socrative, quickly reviews their answers, and in response clarifies any misunderstandings. Later in the unit she asks questions about gut microbiome. Celebratory stickers are given to all on days when 85% get the exit slips correct.

For their performance task, students are assigned roles as doctors who will engineer artificial organs to physically break down food, chemically extract nutrients, absorb the nutrients, and eliminate the remainder. Students are given a set of play teeth, plastic bags, basting and infusing gadgets, various pipes and tubes, playdough, gauze, and paint. They work in small groups, decide each person's role, develop their strategy, and video their work. The assignment is assessed with a rubric that includes labeling of digestive parts, arrangement of parts to serve digestive functions, and explanation of processes. It also includes research, collaboration, problem solving, and innovation. They receive teacher and peer feedback throughout the process, make revisions, and present to a panel of experts such as the school nurse, a nutrition teacher, or family doctor. Feedback is used to revise and improve their model.

At the end of the unit, the summative assessment is a combination of selected choice questions on vocabulary, processes of digestion, interactions of digestive parts, and completion items where students explain and evaluate information. They also write a story about a food's adventure as it moves through the digestive system. They can do this in writing or using presentation software.

In all of these strategies, students are involved, learning is visible, and assessment is purposefully embedded and student focused. For Ms. Sindor the assessments are embedded in learning and at times the assessments are the learning. Think about whether you would know more today about your digestive system if you were assigned a 20-page chapter to study or participated in this type of learning.

Checkpoint on Embedded Assessment

Select a standard or learning target from your grade level or content area. Select two assessments to embed throughout teaching and learning or use as the learning.

Example: For this second grade ELA and Science lesson on gravity, the ELA standard is: "Write informative/explanatory texts in which they introduce a topic, use facts and definitions to develop points, and provide a concluding statement or section." The science standard is: "Students will use the scientific method to test hypotheses about gravity."

Instructional strategies include a self-scored pre-assessment, mini lecture/demonstration and a Bill Nye video with questions embedded via *Zaption*. During learning students predict and explain what happens to falling objects of different mass and weights.

Assessments include students recording information on a learning tracker and writing challenge questions for other groups to answer. Teacher, peer, and self-assessment is frequent. The unit test has sequenced selected choice questions followed by a Dear Voyager letter explaining gravity on our planet or writing a story about what life is like on planets with different gravities.

Higher and Deeper

The enduring ideas of higher level thinking were systemically organized by Benjamin Bloom in 1956, and subsequently revised by Lorin Anderson and David Krathwohl (2001). In both versions higher level thinking includes analysis, evaluation, synthesis, and creating. Norman Webb's Depth of Knowledge (1997) defines levels of thinking from recall to analysis and original ideas. Table 3.4 illustrates how their ideas combine to support both higher and deeper thinking. The darkening background colors show increasingly higher and deeper thinking.

James Pellegrino and Margaret Hilton's report for the The National Academies "Education for Life and Work" (2012, p. 1) define deeper learning as "taking what was learned and applying it to new situations." Tom Vander Ark and Carri Schneider's report (2012) for The William and Flora Hewlett Foundation defines deeper learning as "a set of competencies students must master in order to develop a keen understanding of academic content and apply their knowledge to problems in the classroom and on the job" (p. 3). The implication is that students will use their learning to evaluate new situations and solve novel problems. Personal qualities (i.e., communication, self-control, and responsibility) and interpersonal skills (i.e., collaboration and leadership) are also essential elements of their definitions.

Table 3.4 Combining Bloom's Taxonomy with Webb's DOK

BLOOM'S TAXONOMY/ WEBB'S DOK	REMEMBER	UNDERSTAND	APPLY	ANALYZE	EVALUATE	CREATE
LEVEL 1 Recall and reproduction	Recall, identify, recognize					
LEVEL 2 Apply skills / knowledge, use, follow procedures		Describe, explain, summarize, identify main ideas	Demonstrate, calculate, change, produce	Explain why, explore, consider, illustrate		
LEVEL 3 Strategic thinking, plan, justify		Connect concepts using supporting evidence.	Research/ solve a novel problem	Contrast, examine, distinguish between, interpret author's purpose	Appraise, verify, present a logical argument to a problem	Brainstorm ideas for alternative solutions
LEVEL 4 Extended thinking, analysis, process multiple conditions		Develop generalizations	Choose from alternatives, solve a problem, revise, work with others to reach goal	Analyze multiple sources of evidence and complex themes	Synthesize information from multiple sources, justify	Design, assemble, formulate, construct a new …

Pathways to Deeper and Higher Learning

Drilling down into a topic in order to understand its core as well as its magnitude means not only learning new concepts but also linking them to known ideas and using them in original ways. Navigating by the stars, then using a map and compass, and finally a GPS leads to deeper understanding and the design of a better path through the labyrinth.

Reaching beyond conventional knowledge means applying learning to unknown situations, dilemmas, and complex questions. This process typically results in products, outcomes, and ideas that go beyond the expected or customary. To do this, students must be supported in using new learning to analyze data, make a critical judgment, or create a novel solution to a problem.

Authentic products and performances such as strategies to reduce world hunger, planning schools of the future, or curating a virtual art portfolio support these outcomes. This is possible at all levels of learning as I saw in one school where the second graders solved the dilemma of the morning bus bottleneck by explaining how to redraw the lines in the parking lot.

These challenges compel students to stretch beyond their current skills and knowledge. At the same time, going outside one's comfort zone requires a secure safety net. It requires trust that no one will laugh at their ideas for a future mode of transportation or the bioengineering of teleportation.

Assessing Deeper and Higher

With higher levels of thinking students reach into new and unfamiliar capabilities. With deeper learning they become inquirers, investigators, and producers. Both of these go beyond routine assessments of learning. But, how can we challenge teachers, schools, and learners to reach higher and deeper?

Around the country there are exemplars of schools that raise students' thinking to higher levels. You may have heard about some of these examples: Big Picture, Expeditionary, Project-based, Envision, New Tech, High Tech, and Renaissance. They all share these common elements:

Table 3.5 Taking Learning and Assessing to Higher Levels

Learning context	Lower order assessment	Higher and deeper assessment
Reading: *The Hungry Caterpillar*	What foods did the caterpillar eat? Why did he get a tummy ache?	What do you recommend he eat so as not to get a tummy ache? Explain why
Early writing—story about two friends arguing	What did you like about his story?	How/why would you rewrite the ending to solve the problem differently?
Graphing	Create a graph of money spent on junk food	Recommend ways to change spending that would reshape the graph
Real-world issues: Food labels	Read 3 food labels to determine the nutrient contribution. Pick the healthiest and explain why	Design a food and its label that meets our class's new and improved nutrition guidelines
Hypothesis	Predict what will happen in a given experiment	Design/conduct an experiment to prove a hypothesis. Make a video of your work
School culture—bullying	List all the ways our school can reduce bullying	Develop an anti-bullying campaign and carry it out in your community. Spread the word through social media
Mindset and motivation	Explain Carol Dweck's theory; include examples	Strategize ways to change your classmates' mindset and increase their motivation

◆ Engaging students in interdisciplinary work built on clear and rigorous goals;

◆ supporting students in developing skills for lifelong learning;

◆ providing opportunities for solving real-world problems;

◆ involving students in presenting their work in public forums;

◆ incorporating a multiplicity of learning outcomes: products (objects, artifacts, creations, models, games), performances (demonstrations), portfolios (collections); and

◆ demonstrating and assessing deeper and higher learning outcomes such as analyzing reasoning, solving, and creating.

These schools typically use instructional methods and assessment strategies that go beyond lower levels of the taxonomy and DOK. Table 3.5 shows some examples for making this transition to higher and deeper learning.

Assessment is intrinsically linked to higher thinking and deeper learning. When students set their own goals they take ownership of learning. When students track their own learning they monitor growth. Using embedded assessments they identify misunderstandings and gaps. This in turn informs and supports their next steps. The result is an ongoing cycle of intentional learning, monitoring, and planning towards higher levels.

Checkpoint on Assessing Higher and Deeper Learning

There are many ways to assess beyond the traditional selected choice, completion, and essay questions.

Step 1: Consider how you could use these learning processes and strategies to develop your students' higher and deeper thinking:

◆ re-enact an ending to a story;
◆ create a quiz show or electronic game;
◆ graphically display complex ideas;
◆ participate in a Socratic Seminar;
◆ produce a podcast;
◆ hold a mock trial; or
◆ design a website to persuade an audience.

Step 2: Combine the learning process with these recommended assessment strategies:

◆ student contracts describing their planned learning outcomes, process, and measures;
◆ detailed checklist for a presentation;
◆ metacognitions and self-reflections on the learning process and outcomes;

- structured peer review that is aligned with project requirements;
- learning logs and anecdotal records of steps taken, learning outcomes, and demonstrations of proficiency;
- rubrics that are adequately detailed and aligned with the task; and
- portfolios that incorporate measures of growth.

Table 3.6 Aligning Higher Level Standards with Learning and Assessment

Learning outcomes	Learning processes	Assessment strategies
Standard: Participate effectively in a range of conversations and collaborations with diverse partners, building on others' ideas and expressing your own clearly and persuasively	**Socratic Seminar:** A formal discussion of selected resources using open-ended questions	See Table 3.7 for a peer assessment of the seminar and Table 3.8 for a student's summative assessment
Add your own standards here:		

To reiterate, always start with the standards. But what about those that aren't measured on standardized tests. The list below shows some standards that are not measured in large-scale tests. Table 3.6 shows a standard in practice during a Socratic Seminar. You can add your ideas for assessing an untested standard in the boxes below the example. Table 3.7 shows an example of an annotated peer review during the Socratic Seminar, and Table 3.8 shows the teacher's summative assessment of each student's participation.

1. Use various types of reasoning (inductive, deductive, etc.) as appropriate to the situation.
2. Respond to the varying demands of audience, task, purpose, and discipline.

Table 3.7 Socratic Seminar: Peer Review Annotation

Person observed	Respectful of others' ideas	Participates equitably, takes turns	Familiar with texts, cites sources	Listens attentively, asks questions	Appropriate use of language	Comments

Table 3.8 Socratic Seminar: Summative Rubric

	Exemplary	Proficient	Developing	Room to grow
Demeanor	Respectful, takes turns, patient, reflective	Generally shows composure and tolerance for diverse ideas	Believes his ideas are the most important to be heard	Frequently impatient and/or disrespectful
Participation	Shows initiative, brings others into the conversation	Engaged and appropriate to the discussion	Reluctant to participate, expresses incomplete ideas	Absorbed in his own ideas. Unable to relate to others' thoughts
Knowledge	Thoroughly familiar with source material	Shows an understanding of the source material	Demonstrates cursory knowledge of the topic	Little or no evidence of preparation
Listening/ questioning	Pays attention, asks clarifying questions, thoughtfully responds	Asks and responds to questions appropriately	Has difficulty paying attention and misunderstands questions	Distracted and uninvolved
Speech and language	Clear, precise, and highly focused	Accurate and fitting to the discussion	At times is unclear or has difficulty in expressing ideas	Makes a number of unclear or unrelated comments

3. Construct viable arguments and critique the reasoning of others.

4. Conduct research projects based on focused questions.

5. Evaluate the argument and claims in relation to the sufficiency of evidence.

6. Integrate and evaluate information presented in diverse media formats.

7. Produce effective communication through multiple mediums: oral, written, visual, non-verbal, and technological.

8. Participate effectively in a range of conversations and collaborations with diverse partners, building on others' ideas and expressing their own clearly and persuasively.

Releasing Responsibility

Douglas Fisher and Nancy Frey (2008; 2013) describe a process for the gradual release of responsibility for learning from the teacher to the student this way: "Gradual release of responsibility recognizes the recursive nature of learning and has teachers cycle purposefully through purpose setting and guided instruction, collaborative learning, and independent experiences" (2013, p. 12). Their model shown in Figure 3.2 depicts the release of responsibility through a process of the teacher regulating learning, then learning together through guided instruction, followed by collaborative practice, and finally independent learning.

The Fisher and Frey model is relevant to assessment in that it has the potential to use a spectrum of assessment strategies, incorporates informative assessments, customizes the release of responsibility to learners, and engages them in a metacognitive process.

In Figure 3.3 below the gradual release of responsibility and ownership of assessment from the teacher to the student requires a similar process. This starts with student-determined goals, planned performances, multiple measures, informed adjustments to learning, and self-monitoring.

Figure 3.2 Gradual Release of Responsibility for Learning

Reprinted with permission of ASCD, Copyright 2014, *Better Learning Through Structured Teaching: A Framework for the Gradual Release of Responsibility, 2nd Edition* (Figure 1.1, p. 3) by Douglas Fisher and Nancy Frey — Alexandria, VA: ASCD, 2014

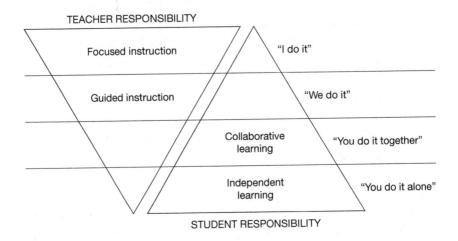

TEACHER RESPONSIBILITY

Focused instruction — "I do it"

Guided instruction — "We do it"

Collaborative learning — "You do it together"

Independent learning — "You do it alone"

STUDENT RESPONSIBILITY

Figure 3.3 Gradual Release of Responsibility for Assessment

From the teacher
- Determines the learning targets
- Plans instructional strategies
- Select criteria for assessment
- Plans and designs the assessments
- Delivers the assessments: Scores and reports the outcomes

To the student
- Sets goals for learning
- Identifies strategies for achieving them
- Chooses how to demonstrate learning
- Establishes assessment criteria
- Monitors learning and self-assesses

Via gradual release
- Students define goals collaboratively
- Develop skills in selecting learning strategies
- Learn multiple ways to demonstrate proficiency
- Guided in making informed corrections
- Supported as self-monitors and reporters of outcomes

Chapter Summary

Key Ideas

1. Assessments are the bonding agents of learning. We don't learn it until we do and show it.

2. Assessment is motivational when it is relevant to the learning, attention-grabbing, and meaningful to the student.

3. Engaging learners in the process empowers them as assessors.

4. Choice, goal setting, self-monitoring, reasonable challenge, and a focus on growth are essential elements of sticky assessment.

5. Assessment must be flexible in order to meet the needs of the learner.

6. Flexibility is achieved through differentiation of content, process, and product.

7. Embedded assessments support a range of learning outcomes.

8. Blending assessment with learning requires using a variety of strategies throughout instruction.

9. Embedded assessments can stretch students to higher and deeper levels of learning.

10. A gradual release of responsibility for assessment is managed through a series of steps that support students as assessors.

Why This Works

Learning is a dynamic process. As knowledge and skills develop, the brain is actively connecting neurons. Sitting, listening, and competing worksheets do not do this as well as participatory learning. Classroom assessments can connect and personalize in ways that standardized tests cannot. Even with computer-adaptive tests, the questions and content are still similar for all learners, only adjusted for level of difficulty. Assessment, like learning, must be personally meaningful and actively engaging in order to make learning last.

Assessments can also provide necessary breaks in learning to give the brain time to recalibrate. Spacing and timing of assessment are essential to embedding learning. No one can memorize Shakespeare's sonnets or the entire periodic table at once. Sorting the elements, playing games, and using rhymes can support this, followed by short quizzes requiring learners to interpret the meaning of the table's design. Applying learning to the creation of a new element supports higher and deeper learning. Students can then present their ideas for review and feedback. For the teacher, this type of assessment makes visible each student's analysis of the feasibility of the creation. Students can solve problems that scientists face, or even write problems for others to solve. All of these make assessment sticky through a repetitive cycle of learn-practice-assess.

These explanations are based on the knowledge that action is more memorable than inaction; doing is more reinforcing than sitting; multimodal assessment is more sticky than just listening. Chunking learning and checking for understanding before moving forward builds the foundations of learning. Ongoing assessment guides decisions about the next steps in teaching and learning.

When we learn a new skill such as driving, no one is allowed to hop in the car, turn on the engine, and head down the freeway. Learners start with an expert beside them and then experience a gradual release of responsibility via practice with parents, until after many months they are allowed to drive on their own. This happens only after the driver has provided evidence of progress towards proficiency and proof of competence.

When you want to make assessment sticky, start each lesson with a review of previous learning and end each lesson with a summary that encourages higher and deeper thinking. Often, teachers jump right into teaching, but focusing on the student's starting and ending points provides better alignment with the measures of learning and more accurate assessment of learning outcomes and growth.

Learning can be supported by chunking content, using memory devices such as mnemonics and reinforcing learning with personal connections and examples. Ask students to transfer learning to another situation such as how does this treaty relate to a war we studied earlier, or how is this character like the one in another book we read? Support higher level thinking by asking students to synthesize or evaluate information as if they were talking to a visitor from Xenon who has no knowledge of the topic. The evidence that is generated is then used to make better decisions about next steps in teaching and learning.

Assessment not only measures and reports learning, but more importantly supports it. Large-scale assessments have a place as part of the picture of a student's learning but are impersonal and less informative to daily learning whereas classroom assessments are better suited to improving student learning through frequent measures, personalization, and immediate responses.

If our goal is student, teacher, and school success, it makes sense to start with assessment success.

Reflection and Application

You can probably remember what Roy G. Biv stands for as well as when Columbus sailed the ocean blue. But there is also much that has been forgotten about Ohm's Law and Greek gods.

Reflection on Sticky Assessment

Think about why and strategies you could use to embed more complex learning. Plan to use sticky assessment:

1. Select a unit of instruction _____
2. List 3 learning targets _____
3. Describe 2 informative assessments _____
4. Describe 2 ways to ways to differentiate assessment
   _____
5. Explain two embedded assessments _____

- What forces are in place moving you towards sticky assessment?
- What forces are holding you back? What can you do about them?
- What are your take-aways? How would you explain this to another teacher, or maybe a Martian?

4

Technically Sound Assessment

Objectives in this chapter

1. Recognize indicators of validity.
2. Take steps to ensure that assessments are reliable.
3. Confirm that assessments are fair for all learners.
4. Seek to enhance balance in assessment.

Foundations of High-Quality Assessment

Some time ago I began compiling all that I could find about the standards for assessment. I used the NCATE standards (National Council for Accreditation of Teacher Education) that are now called CAEP (Council for the Accreditation of Educator Preparation), the NCME (National Council on Measurement in Education), and publications on the assessment of students from American Federation of Teachers and National Education Association. By far the most comprehensive came from JCSEE (The Joint Committee on Standards for Educational Evaluation). JCSEE is an educational cooperative that includes AERA (American Educational Research Association), APA (American Psychological Association), CCSSO (Council of Chief State School Officers), NAESP (National Association of Elementary School Principals),

NASSP (National Association of Secondary School Principals), NCME (National Center for Measurement in Education), NSBA (National School Board Association), and others.

More recently "Criteria for High-Quality Assessment" was published by a partnership between SCOPE (Stanford Center for Opportunity Policy in Education), CRESST (National Center for Research on Student Standards and Testing), and the Learning Sciences Research Institute (Darling-Hammond, Herman, Pellegrino, et al., 2013).

The European Framework of Standards for Educational Assessment (AEA, 2012) was published by the Association for Educational Assessment – Europe. Their document includes recommendations for research-supported assessment practices and systems.

Despite all our efforts to make assessment an exact science, there still remains a significant element of professional judgment and decision making. "Understanding this underlying assumption helps teachers and administrators realize the importance of their own judgments and those of others in evaluating the quality of the assessment and the meaning of the results" (McMillan, 2000).

There are commonalities among all these standards in relation to the technical accuracy of assessment. In this section you will find a synthesis of the key ideas with each unpacked and elaborated in relation to their application in schools and classrooms. It is not only in high-stakes testing, but also in daily practice that assessment must be technically sound in order to make learning purposeful and teaching responsive.

Valid

Validity refers to how well or accurately an instrument is measuring what it claims to be measuring. It also means that the inferences and decisions being made are sound and accurate. On the surface, validity means that the strategy measures the intentions of the assessment. It is easy to ask whether the vocabulary test showed that students mastered the unit terminology at a predetermined level of achievement at a selected moment in learning. It is harder to determine this with more complex and higher level learning such as a synthesis of ideas or creation of an original product. The result is that while standardized tests can measure recall, understanding, and application they are not a valid way to assess analysis, evaluation, and producing.

A second element of validity is the precision of the assessment. This refers to the quality of the measure being used. I still remember a third grade test where I was asked how high the seat of a chair is (no particular chair was identified). I pondered a kitchen chair, my father's easy chair, or my little sister's chair and still do not know the answer to that question.

Checkpoint on Validity

In the two sets of questions below, which do you think is a more accurate measure of understanding the sequence of photosynthesis?

Multiple choice

Write the letter of the correct answer in the space before the question.

1. In the process of photosynthesis the plant absorbs the sunlight first because

    A: If it was last, we would have backwards plants
    B: The plant needs sunlight before it can produce food
    C: Our book says it happens that way
    D: In the movie we watched we saw one plant grown in the dark and another grown in the light.

Fill-in

2. Use the descriptions below to place the five steps in the correct order

A	D	C	B	E
First Step	Second Step	Third Step	Fourth Step	Fifth Step

Phrase Bank:

A. Chloroplasts absorb and trap sunlight
B. Light energy, water, minerals and carbon dioxide combine to produce food in the form of sugar (glucose) for the plant
C. Water and minerals flow from the roots up the stem to the leaf
D. Carbon dioxide enters the leaf through the stomata
E. Oxygen leaves the leaf through the stomata

Correct sequence: A, C, D, B, E

Which question is a more valid and accurate assessment? Why?

The third element of valid assessment is that the inferences being made about the learner are accurate. It is the interpretation of test results that guides our decisions about grouping, placement, advancement, and more. These decisions can result in unintended and even intended but dreadful consequences for schools and students. Grant Wiggins (2014) explains that this results in "people bashing test questions without understanding, supervisors giving inadequate advice, and teachers designing invalid tests without realizing it."

Accurate interpretation depends on other factors such as whether the assessments match the instruction and learning targets and also how well the student understands the question. Can we infer that Shabina failed the multiple choice question because she wasn't able to calculate the area of a rectangular prism or because of a limitation in understanding the language? A prism, to some, represents a three-dimensional triangular shape that refracts light. However, in geometry it describes a three-dimensional object whose six sides are rectangles. The use of different measures and types of evidence can bolster the validity of students' test scores.

Validity also takes into account how well the content of the assessment aligns with what you intend to assess. Ms. McGoom wants to measure the learning that occurred during a project on planetary orbits. In the unit, students read about planets, watched a video, and acted as planets in orbit. She is given a unit test by the grade level coordinator and asks if it is okay to add some higher level questions to the test. She is given the go-ahead and in addition to the selected choice and completion questions on planets, orbits, and gravitational pull, she gives the students a choice of case studies. In one the students are scientists trying to figure out why one planet has gone rogue and is out of its regular orbit. Students are required to posit and explain their reasoning. In the other a scientist is claiming that the orbit of the planet they have been studying is speeding up; students are to explain whether this can or cannot happen and why.

A multistep problem reduces validity when it is hard to determine in which step the error was made. For example: Heraldo sells his paintings at the local art gallery. He gets $29.50 for a large watercolor picture and $12.95 for a smaller oil painting. Last month he sold six large and two small paintings. How much did he make for the month? Under these circumstances it is hard to tell whether he had difficulty in multiplication, addition, or vocabulary.

Once data is gathered it is important to piece it together in order to get a complete picture of a student's learning. If a teacher wants to use multiple measures, he must be certain that each measure is assessing what it intends to measure. For example, during a unit on Early Explorers in which learners read different books and source materials it is important that each report or presentation considers the same content such as the biographical information, education, people who influenced them, and discoveries. Once all students have a shared foundation of knowledge, they can elaborate on their learning and present it through multiple channels.

Grant Wiggins (2014) also explains an interesting phenomenon when he says "a question can seem trivial or odd but provide valid inferences against the learning goal just as there can be questions that seem profound and illuminating but are invalid for use with the goal." For example, if we want to determine a fifth grader's ability to construct an essay, but ask them to write about the politics of a government shutdown, are we measuring their knowledge of current events or their writing ability?

Validity is not only about the instruction but rather the accuracy of the inferences drawn from the assessments and the consequences resulting from them. When considering the validity of an assessment keep in mind these key elements and processes:

◆ be certain that the learning targets are clearly defined and are measurable;

◆ determine how closely the assessment aligns with the learning targets and the instruction;

◆ provide multiple tasks that require students to show understanding of the topic rather than just memorization of learning;

◆ provide tasks that make thinking visible;

◆ avoid unrelated information such as prior knowledge that is required for success on the current assessment;

◆ work with another educator to review your assessments;

◆ plan assessment processes, products, and strategies using an assessment blueprint or map in order to be sure that varied types and levels of thinking are being assessed and integrated throughout teaching and learning;

◆ use scoring criteria that match the purpose and learning outcomes; and

◆ compare pre- to post-scores to determine growth on specified learning outcomes.

Through the use of valid practices, the effects of unintended consequence of the assessment can be avoided. In this way all students have the same opportunities for success.

Reliable

Reliability refers to the consistency of the outcomes across time, population, and place. It means that the assessments are free from error, the directions are clear, and content and processes have been taught. When an assessment is reliable, we can be more confident that whoever is giving the test and wherever it may be given, the results will be constant. Users of the assessment information must be able to rely on the data generated by assessments even when they take place in different classrooms or even in different schools, states, and countries on different days. Teachers giving the same grade level common assessment should know beforehand whether the content has clearly been taught, strategies are valid and thus the results are reliable and consistent across classrooms.

If a unit of instruction is on characterization with a learning target on discerning flat from round characters, a reliable question used by multiple teachers may ask about which character(s) fit into each category, accompanied by an explanation of why the student put them there. Alternatively a student could be asked to provide two examples from the story where Crash Coogan displayed growth in his moral understanding. Reliability is reduced when students are asked to interpret the author's purpose in describing the character as irresponsible in that students may agree or disagree with this premise and teachers may interpret their response from their own perspectives.

To be sure that they are measuring the full range of learning targets in the poetry unit, the fifth grade teachers design a comprehensive test blueprint. Their learning targets are:

◆ define the elements of different types of poems;
◆ interpret a variety of types of figurative language; and
◆ produce a portfolio of original poetry that represents different styles.

For their assessment, students are given selected choice questions asking them to identify elements of poetry such as "The moon shone like a great big yellow pie in the night sky" and categorizing different types of poems. Students also submit their writer's notebook where they have created examples of different types of poems: haiku, cinquain, limerick, etc. The scoring of the notebooks is based on a rubric of their analysis of the poems: constructed accurately and labeled correctly, the types of poems are explained and elements of poetry identified.

Reliability can be compromised when there are time pressures to complete an entire test during a specified period of time. When test anxiety goes up, reliability goes down. On any given day a student may be more or less alert, sick or healthy, and have variations in ability to concentrate. All of these have an impact on our ability to ensure consistency of results. To meet this requirement, the grade level teachers give the test in parts and have students write and collect their poems throughout the unit. They also compare the data from the unit pretest to examine specific areas of growth. They note one question that students consistently got wrong on both measures. It was a question about foreshadowing and they decide to review that concept with this year's classes and teach it more purposefully next year.

Keep in mind that reliability is more influenced by student factors than is validity. If students are hungry, in poor health, or anxious, their scores can vary. This is why many schools provide breakfast and engage students in an activity that might distract, calm, or pick up the pace before they take a test.

When considering reliability, keep in mind these key factors:

- be sure that directions and questions are fully clear;
- provide an adequate number of questions for each learning target;
- assess each learning target using varied assessment strategies;
- offer differentiated or adaptive testing;
- reduce subjectivity in grading through scoring keys and rubrics; and
- work with another educator to review your assessments.

Fair

The question of fairness has plagued testing since its early days. In relation to fairness, the most commonly discussed ideas relate to bias and stereotypes. It can also apply to inequity and favoritism as well as unfair penalties, outcomes, and decisions that result from the assessment. Is it possible to design an assessment that works for all learners, in all situations? Yes, there are strategies that can make assessment fairer if not flawless for every student. What is most important is to ensure that all students receive fair treatment and that no student's opportunities are limited due to a test.

Linda Suskie (2000) explains that students should be given equitable opportunities to demonstrate what they know. This means that "students are assessed using methods and procedures most appropriate to them, depending on the students' prior knowledge, cultural experience, and cognitive style. Creating custom-tailored assessments for each student is, of course, largely impractical, but nevertheless there are steps we can take to make our assessment methods as fair as possible."

Mr. Nehishi's class recently finished a unit about how foods reflect culture. In small mixed groups, students researched and presented on food and culture from Asian, African, Latino, European, and other cultures. At the conclusion of the unit, the test included mostly selected choice questions primarily on Asian and Latino food and culture. This was very advantageous for some students but not for others. In addition, most of the questions were based on remembering and understanding rather than a comparison of the multiple influences on eating patterns. Clearly it would have been fairer to include questions about a variety of cultures or give students an opportunity to select cultures for comparison, nutritional analysis, and factors influencing eating patterns.

Another aspect of fairness is in relation to students' preparation for the assessment. Have they been provided with the knowledge and skills necessary to be successful? A test based solely on the textbook is different from one that is a reflection of students' presentations or teacher-provided resources. A common plaint from older students is that they studied from the teacher's notes or memorized the 50 facts that they were led to believe were important and then found the test was a set of problems to solve.

Students also need to know the types of assessments that will be used to measure their knowledge, understanding, and skills. Students' chances of success will vary depending on whether they are required to take a selected choice test where there is one right answer or whether they can use their learning to explain and support their beliefs about Christopher Columbus or an historic event. Fairness also means that all students have access to sufficient and relevant resources. If an assignment requires online reading it is essential that all students have access to technology.

In Practice

Consider the fairness factor in these examples.

Carlson is able to verbally predict the outcome of 100 dice tosses and he can verbally explain his thinking; however, he is unable to explain his solution in writing or with a mathematical algorithm. How can his teacher be fair in assessing his knowledge of probability?

What about Anika who is trying to understand these homophone sentences:

◆ The school **principal** has very high **principles**
◆ Our **mail** is delivered by a **male**
◆ When the pitcher **threw** the ball, the catcher rolled **through** the mud to get it.

How should we score her when she uses the word correctly but misspells it?

In the books, *Huckleberry Finn* and *Tom Sawyer*, the Duke and the Dauphin are

A: Actors   B: Beggars   C: Bankers   D: Charlatans.

This question could be considered unfair because a student needs to know the higher grade level vocabulary term in choice D.

How fair is it to give a multicultural class words that are the same in English and Spanish such as *bonanza, armadillo, flotilla,* and *vamoose* versus words that would be more challenging for all learners such as *remittance, deluge, secede,* and *succeed*?

When considering fairness, keep these ideas in mind:

- make sure learning targets are clear and visible;
- check that all students understand what they are expected to learn;
- pre-assess for background knowledge and then differentiate content, strategies, pacing, and/or assessments;
- be transparent about the types of assessments that will be used throughout teaching and learning;
- verify that your assessments are fair for all types of learners, learning, and purposes;
- consider differences in background, gender, cultural beliefs, and access to information;
- bias can occur in the context of a task. If the math question is about football and that knowledge or terminology is part of the assessment, then it may be unfair to some learners;
- provide students with sufficient practice prior to the assessment;
- be sure that all students have equivalent opportunities to show their learning;
- emphasize growth over final test scores; and
- recognize that teachers and learners may interpret the questions and results in different ways.

Balanced

When we take into account the validity, reliability, and fairness of an assessment we are more apt to be accurate in our interpretation, conclusions, and inferences. Although validity, fairness, and reliability are the foundations of technically sound assessment, for many educators, balance is the cumulative outcome. Balance means we use an inclusive range of strategies including formative, benchmark, diagnostic, summative, and alternative measures. In addition, the assessments are used at all levels of the education system: national, state, district, school, grade level, classroom, and student.

Can you think of a time when an assessment was valid not reliable? If a student takes an annual test that only measures the last six weeks of the first semester, validity comes into question. This is a situation in which the test is consistently not measuring the full range of taught learning targets. Alternatively it could mean that the students didn't know what they were expected to learn, or how they would be assessed, or were only given one way to show their learning. For example, a test with only word problems in math, may be assessing the learners' language and decoding skills rather than their ability to multiply and divide accurately.

Alternatively, an assessment can be reliable without being valid. Time after time, when you step on the scale, it shows that you have gained 10 pounds, but perhaps the scale needs to be recalibrated so as to make it more accurate in its measure. The measure may be reliable, in that it is consistent, but it is not valid in terms of accurately measuring what it purports to measure. If your doctor used this data to label you obese, the treatment would be different than if you were still within your normal weight range.

In seeking balance in assessment keep in mind these key factors:

- rely on multiple measures so students can show what they know in different ways;
- include a balance of questions and tasks that represent the range of learning targets;
- be clear on your purposes before designing and administering an assessment; and
- consider the consequences of the assessment on teachers and students.

Chapter Summary

Key Ideas

1. Coherent assessments are valid and reliable.
2. Cogent assessments are free from bias and distortion.
3. Usable assessments provide information on specified learning targets.

4. Dependable assessments are those we can count on to provide accurate and consistent information.

5. Assessments that are accurate in their measurement can be used to inform decisions.

6. Assessments must be both reliable and valid: When the results are consistent (reliable), make sure they are also valid in that you are measuring the intended targets.

7. Assessments are fair when they are equitable for all students.

Why This Works

Validity, reliability, fairness, and balance inform many decisions that teachers make about their instructional practices and their students. When teachers share data they can better determine students' strengths and respond to learning gaps. Continuous use and responsiveness to data from all types of assessments guides informed responses. Time and opportunities to collect, analyze, and discuss information on learning outcomes are essential.

1. When the content of the test matches what was taught we can make accurate assumptions about students.

2. When we can make accurate assumptions, our responses are more likely to be appropriate and relevant for the learner.

3. Clear directions support learners in understanding what is expected of them on the assessment.

4. We live in an increasingly diverse world thus the elimination of all types of bias is essential.

5. Learners must be provided with knowledge, skills, and tools to foster their success on various assessments.

6. Multiple measures of multiple types of learning provide clearer insights into learning.

7. Assessment informs instruction, instruction informs learners, learners inform teachers.

8. Assessment requires a certain level of professional interpretation and decision making thus the more accurate these are the better students are served.

9. Assessment is a complex conglomeration of measurement, evidence, and interpretation.

"Not everything that can be counted counts, and not everything that counts can be counted." Albert Einstein

Reflection and Application

In your PLC a teacher makes the following statements about validity:

◆ I give frequent mini-quizzes that I score and return the next day.

◆ I give students a weekly summative test on what they have learned.

◆ We review and build a learning mindset with a problem of the day or week.

◆ Homework is routinely checked.

◆ I keep anecdotal evidence of effort and achievement.

How should she respond when her Principal asks about the validity of her classroom assessments?

1. What kind of validity evidence has she obtained?

2. What pitfalls should she avoid so that her inference will be valid?

3. If you were on her learning team, what advice would you give her about strengthening the validity of her practice?

In your PLC a teacher makes the following statements about reliability:

◆ I collaborate with other teachers on developing classroom assessments: We review and check each other's questions.

◆ I match questions to the objectives I have taught. I make sure each objective has been assessed and also that it is assessed at different levels of difficulty.

◆ Over time, I determined that some questions are unfair or not suitable based on students' responses so I removed them from the test.

1. How would you assess her assessment reliability?
2. What recommendations would you make to enhance reliability?

In a post-observation meeting you ask the teacher about the diversity of students in her class and how she makes sure that she is being fair to all students. She says:

◆ Of course it is fair; I use the questions that come with the teacher's guide to our text.

◆ For some students, I have the test translated into their native language.

1. How would you respond to her current approach to fairness?
2. What additional strategies would you recommend to support the fairness of her assessments?

Summary
Endings are New Beginnings

Objectives in this chapter

1. Value and prioritize the multiple purposes of assessment in the service of learning.
2. Balance and utilize all types of assessment.
3. Consider systems and cycles of assessment.
4. Strengthen classroom assessment practices.
5. Develop and promote a culture of assessment.

Returning to the Roots of Assessment

Whenever I come to the end of a trip, I often feel that time has passed much too quickly and there is still much to see and do. During my travels I record experiences in journals and logs, post some for friends and family, and stow others away for further reflection. When I return to cities such as San Francisco or Sydney the anticipation of visiting these places again brings a sense of renewal as these experiences regenerate the excitement I felt the first time and build anticipation of new things to learn and do. It may seem like a stretch to compare travel to assessment, but for me both are journeys without end.

As I look back on previous chapters, I realize that there is much to reflect upon, analyze, evaluate, and take action on. I am heartened when I look at how far we have come in assessment from the days of timed, selected choice bubble sheets, to adaptable and more complex assessment as well as rigorous project-based learning. But we still have far to travel in returning assessment to teachers and learners, in engaging students as assessors, and building confidence in small-scale and local measures of learning. We must continue to push the balance towards using assessment in the service of learning rather than its finish line. Returning to the core of assessment means *assidere*, to sit beside and guide, rather than *expertus*, meaning having been tested or to prove oneself.

Checkpoint on Assessment Literacy

In the introduction to the book, you were asked to reflect on your knowledge and skills of assessment literacy and set goals for mastering the key concepts. Returning to each of the key concepts after reading the book, rate your current skills and knowledge on a 1 to 10 scale with 1 being the lowest and 10 being the highest.

1. Designing and selecting assessment instruments _____
2. Aligning assessment with the desired standards and learning outcomes _____
3. Matching the assessment with the purpose: formative, summative, benchmark _____
4. Utilizing multiple methods to assess diverse levels of cognitive complexity _____
5. Monitoring student progress towards learning targets _____
6. Administering, scoring, and interpreting teacher-produced assessments _____
7. Interpreting assessment data in relation to strengths, gaps, growth, and final outcomes _____
8. Using assessment results when making decisions about individual students, planning, teaching, developing curriculum, and school improvement _____
9. Developing reliable pupil-grading procedures that depend on valid student assessments _____
10. Communicating assessment results to students, parents, and other audiences _____
11. Recognizing unethical, illegal, and inappropriate assessment methods and uses of assessment information _____

- Which practices do you want to strengthen?

- What steps will you take?

Finding Balance

Over the past few decades, assessment has become skewed towards the high-stakes large-scale end of the spectrum. From the teacher who has to defend her growth scores to the one who engages her students in first-rate projects that include precise assessments of content knowledge, deeper understanding, and real-world applications, only to be asked at her annual evaluation only about students' DRP or Dibel scores, we are losing sight of what is really important to learn and assess.

At the same time, we are taking assessment out of the hands of teachers, the people who best know their learners and giving authority to commercial test makers and data managers. A student like Tashi may have been labeled with low level language skills, but unbeknown to the data analyzer, has a range of personal traits such as tenacity and dedication that could overcome any language barriers she may temporarily face in achieving her goals.

There is a place where we find balance between large-scale and local. Examples throughout this book showed the importance of starting off with large-scale standards. But, typically these are not measurable with one small-scale question. Rather, those large standards must be deconstructed so they are teachable and assessable in the classroom. In Chapter 1, Ms. Sindor showed how to deconstruct the common core, blend it with content area and curricular standards, and plan varied instructional routines and assessment strategies.

High-stakes tests cannot capture the full range and intent of large-scale standards. In fact, some of them are not measured at all, for example: "Engage effectively in a range of collaborative discussions with diverse partners on grade level topics." It is in the classroom where teachers are better able to analyze the intent, teach the standard using rich content, and assess with a range of methods including selected choice, completion, problem solving, fact-checked essays, performances, and portfolios of learning. It is in the classroom that students' knowledge and skills, strengths, and learning gaps become evident and teachers can respond in a timely and personalized manner.

Assessment Systems

Local Systems

Large-scale systems have been put in place at the national and state level. The primary emphasis of these systems is on the alignment of standards to test questions and the coherence between the standards and what students are being taught. The primary audience for these are policy managers and data analysts. When scores are delivered numerically to parents and teachers, it is difficult to tell whether a student was tired, had test anxiety, or was simply guessing. However this data is used to determine funding, programming, and staffing. The large-scale responses to large-scale data don't typically consider students' incoming abilities and prior levels of achievement and other locally based mitigating factors between classrooms, schools, and districts.

Elements of an Assessment System

One alternative to the external control is the development of local balanced assessment systems that are comprehensive, purposeful, informative, and responsive. In designing your local system consider how these elements will be put into practice.

Step 1: Clarify your vision and priorities

- Develop a cohesive and actionable mission and purpose for your assessment system.
- Make decisions about what is important and worthy to measure.
- Consider how to assess growth, not solely final scores.

Step 2: Compose an inclusive process

- Engage a wide range of stakeholders.
- Include parents, teachers, students, administrators, funders, and other community members.
- Think comprehensively about assessments that illuminate a spectrum of knowledge, skills, and affect.

Step 3: Design a coherent system

◆ Illuminate learning and assessing in ways that are practical, flexible, and manageable.
◆ Substantiate the validity, reliability, and fairness of assessments.
◆ Take a cyclical approach that seeks to continually improve practice and outcomes.

Step 4: Translate into practice

◆ Design/select a continuum of strategies: formative, diagnostic, benchmark, summative.
◆ Support, coach, and guide teachers in implementing best practices in assessment.
◆ Illuminate strengths; plan for improvement.

Step 5: Foster local ownership

◆ Illuminate the need for action, model commitment.
◆ Affirm the long- and short-term benefits for teachers and learners: consistency, clarity, results.
◆ Continuously review and improve your practice.

Local Assessment Cycle

A transparent process is required for successful implementation. Figure S.1 shows, in brief, a cycle of a local assessment system. Each element can be elaborated, for example, the local mission and beliefs can be explained and described with references and electronic links, the planned assessments identified and posted, and resources on best practice readily available.

The Five Abilities of a Dynamic Assessment System

1. *Account-ability*: The system is feasible to explain to others and practical to monitor by multiple constituents in order to ensure effectiveness and efficiency.
2. *Response-ability*: Individuals, teams, leaders have the knowledge and skills to respond to data that demonstrates progress as well as lingering gaps in order to ensure continuous improvement.

3. *Quantify-ability*: The validity and reliability of both qualitative and quantitative data can be substantiated and responded to in fair and precise ways.
4. *Communic-ability*: Accurate information is disseminated to a broad range of individuals and groups in a way that they can comprehend and utilize it.
5. *Flex-ability*: The system is elastic and adaptable in order to support all learners in reaching their highest levels of achievement.

Figure S.1 Planning a Local Assessment System

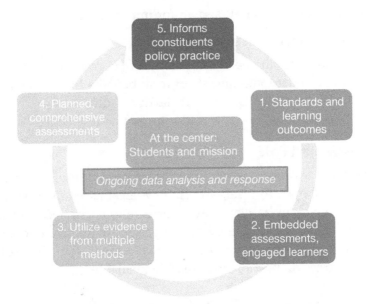

Checkpoint on Assessment Systems: Table S.1

Choose one of the following to apply in your own setting, or alternatively try them all:

5 steps in designing an assessment system;
5 steps in the assessment cycle;
5 assessment abilities.

Table S.1 Taking Action on Your Assessment Systems

Step or practice or action	Application to your school or setting

Strengthening Classroom Assessment

I recently watched *Words and Pictures*, a movie about two teachers feuding over which was mightier, the pen or the brush. After much squabbling they concluded that words and pictures are both important. It made me think about arguments over what types of tests and measures are the best. I hope you agree that multiple measures throughout all levels of the taxonomy and depth of learning are essential to today's learners in the complex world which they are growing into.

Supporting Teachers

Having worked with many teachers in numerous districts, I believe that teachers are among the most dedicated and compassionate professionals I have ever met. They look for the best in their students, persevere through numerous challenges, manage class-rooms that are respectful and inclusive, model excellence in content knowledge and instructional methodology, and continuously seek out opportunities for growth and improvement. They do not need to be herded into a workshop to listen for hours to less than relevant instruction on a new computer system that is promised to make their data management easier.

Rather what teachers need is to feel that their skills and knowledge are valued, their ability to meet the needs of diverse learners is appreciated, their inclusion of parents and the community is respected, and that when their work results in student growth, they will have a job for one more year. They need support and guidance as they are teaching, opportunities to work with their peers on improvements to teaching, learning, and assessing, and just-in-time learning of the knowledge and skills required to be effective classroom assessors.

Stuart Kahl (2010) explains that "New curricular emphases, programs, and instructional techniques have come and gone. But rather than seeing gargantuan improvements in student achievement, the small gains in large-scale assessment results have been far from adequate. If one accepts that interactions between students and teachers are the key to significant improvements in student achievement, then it becomes obvious where we should focus attention—on teaching and assessment practices that have been shown to lead to real improvement" (p. 1).

Teachers wear many hats and the assessment one is their most important. This requires an adjustment in mindset throughout all levels of assessment from policy and teacher preparation to classroom practice:

◆ from a focus on numerical measures of learning to assessment of quality of learning;
◆ from emphasizing planning to understanding learning;
◆ from reliance on textbooks to assessing students' ability to analyze all types of texts;
◆ from traditional measures to alternative and authentic measures of learning;
◆ from specified testing times to ongoing formative assessment;
◆ from reliance on provided tests to confidence in development of local assessments; and

◆ from using tests to calculate final grades to relying on assessments to support learning.

Developing Students

Strengthening and supporting teachers as assessors is enhanced when they work in partnership with their students. In the classroom, assessments serve many purposes. A pre-assessment or one midway through instruction provides information on where students are headed, what is expected, and where they are in relation to the learning objectives. Although formative assessments are generally not counted towards grades they can guide teachers in adapting pacing, depth, content, resources, and more. Students can gain insights into how they are progressing and what they can do to improve.

It is in the classroom that students can become effective self-assessors when they compare their work to exemplars. Through precision rubrics they can self-reflect before submitting for peer or teacher review. They can track their progress towards learning targets and even adjust and personalize their own goalposts and products.

James McMillan and Jessica Hearn (2008) say that "Correctly implemented student self-assessment can promote intrinsic motivation, internally controlled effort, a mastery goal orientation, and more meaningful learning" (p. 40).

Checkpoint on Valuing and Upskilling Assessment Practice

Table S.2 Upskilling Assessment Practice

My current practices and beliefs	What I would like to upskill

Consider something you are doing now in your classroom in relation to assessment. Think about ways to improve and advance your practice, your beliefs about assessment, or engaging learners as assessors.

Fostering a Culture of Assessment

Once a school or district has formed a vision of assessment through a collaboratively developed, balanced, and aligned system the next step is to cultivate an assessment-based classroom culture. In these settings students feel safe taking opportunities to stretch their learning. They have multiple ways to show what they know and are supported in their growth.

Teachers in this culture know that their evaluation is not based solely on one annual test. They know that their rigorous and purposeful classroom assessments yield valuable insights into student learning. There is an atmosphere of collegiality and cooperation where best practices are openly shared and each learner is nurtured towards their potential. This is a place where assessment is done right.

Prerequisites to Change

Nobody knows what the future might bring. Perhaps robots will replace teachers or knowledge will be inserted directly into the brain through vectors or headbands. Whatever the future may look like, the research is clear that assessment is an integral and ongoing part of teaching and learning.

What we do know about assessment is that it is most valuable when it is closest to the source of learning, the teachers and students, and that it can be acted on expediently and accurately. We know what practices are most effective: Clear targets, formative assessment, descriptive feedback, student engagement, and numerous others described throughout this book.

Large-scale assessments provide a snapshot of a student learning in a moment in time. When we look at the big picture it becomes evident that not everyone is succeeding, scores have only slightly edged up, and with each new iteration we start over with new baselines.

An effective culture of assessment means that assessment is valued as a process throughout teaching and learning, assessment strategies and learning outcomes are visible, and classrooms are safe places to make mistakes. Teachers are well informed and supported in using best practice and school leadership encourages their growth through a wide range of measures of success. This is a local culture rather than one imposed from outside the school.

"It is insufficient to simply point out right and wrong answers. For assessment to be informative students must hold a similar concept of quality as the teacher, be able to compare their current performance with the standard, and be able to take action to close the gap" (Shepard, 2005, p. 68).

To support this mindset, we need to make certain that new teachers are competent classroom assessors and at the same time provide ongoing support to in-service teachers that will enable them to remain current on research and best practice.

Measuring what matters means determining the most important learning outcomes. There is a lot of talk about critical thinking, innovation, collaboration, personal responsibility, but as long as the tests measure discrete facts about reading, writing, and math they are sending a message that "retrieval and procedural application of narrow skills and facts is what counts as useful learning" (Schwartz and Arena, 2013, p. 5). When we truly value more complex skills, then we can change assessments to measure what is truly meaningful and useful.

Restorative Assessment

Restorative assessment is a process of returning assessment to its established purposes and substantiated processes. When we sit beside our students we can verify that the assessments are fair and balanced rather than a reflection of a student's zip-code. Restoring balance means stopping the increasingly rapid pendulum swings in search of making schools uniform, teaching unvarying, and learners homogeneous. It means going in the opposite direction to support learning, improve deep understanding, and make learning relevant for all learners.

Imbalance is similar to a tire where the center of rotation is different from the center of gravity resulting in vibration, pulling to one side, and uneven wear. Over time, it can affect and damage other parts of your car. Large-scale assessment is like a static balance where the tire is placed on a fulcrum and weights are placed to reduce the disequilibrium. With dynamic assessment, the balancing is a simulation of actual conditions where misaligned points are adjusted purposefully. In a dynamic classroom process, teaching builds on prior learning, assessment is a continuous process, and multiple methods are used for measuring and reporting.

Restorative assessment includes the following:

◆ assess learning in all subjects and content areas – this includes the arts, technical areas, and vocational subjects;
◆ use multiple measures to triangulate learning and support all types of learners;
◆ provide multiple ways for students to show what they know;
◆ report learning outcomes using a balanced measure of progress and outcomes;
◆ restore the focus on assessment for and as learning;
◆ balance large-scale and local, summative and formative;
◆ build teachers' proficiency in planning, utilizing, and responding to classroom assessment; and
◆ refocus on assessment from procedural steps to practical skills for the real world.

In Closing

Perhaps you read this book for personal growth or maybe it was a required reading. As you look back on those aha! moments, or had thoughts about changes you would like to make in your practice, think about your personal take-aways. Also consider those ideas you want to share with other educators who you can depend on to give you valuable feedback and continuously enrich your thoughts and actions.

Take a moment to reflect on your upskilled beliefs, knowledge, and competencies. Then write a note to yourself in response to these prompts you considered in the preface:

◆ How have your beliefs about the process and purpose of assessment changed?

◆ What assessment practices will you change? Consider the value of alignment, using assessment informatively, making learning stick, and technically sound practice.

◆ What new ideas do you have for gathering, using, and responding to data?

◆ What changes will you make to your professional learning and growth to best support your knowledge and skills as an assessment leader?

◆ Why do you think this works? Why or when might it not work?

◆ What are your lingering questions?

◆ What are your next steps to fulfill your vision of best practice in local assessment?

References

Anderson, L.W. and Krathwohl, D.R. (2001). *A Taxonomy for Learning, Teaching, and Assessing: A revision of Bloom's taxonomy and educational objectives*. New York: Longman.

Andrade, H., Huff, K., and Brooke, G. (2012). *Assessing Learning. Students at the Center: Teaching and learning in the era of the common core*. Job for the Future. Available at: www.studentsatthecenter. org/topics/assessing-learning. Accessed on December 12, 2015.

APA, AERA, NCME (2014). *Standards for Educational and Psychological Testing*. Available at: www.aera.net/Publications/Books/Standards forEducationalPsychologicalTesting(2014Edition)/tabid/15578/ Default.aspx. Accessed on May 4, 2015.

Association for Educational Assessment (AEA) – Europe. (2012). *European Framework of Standards for Educational Assessment*. Available at: www.aea-europe.net/images/downloads/SW_ Framework_of_European_Standards.pdf. Accessed on January 12, 2016.

Black, P. and Wiliam, D. (2009). "Developing the theory of formative assessment." *Educational Assessment, Evaluation and Accountability*, 21 (1), pp. 5–31.

Black, P., Harrison, C., Lee, C., Marshall, B., and Wiliam, D. (2002). "Working Inside the Black Box: Assessment for learning in the classroom." *Phi Delta Kappan*, 86 (1), pp. 8–21.

Bloom, B. S. (1971). "Mastery learning." In J. H. Block (Ed.), *Mastery Learning: Theory and practice* (pp. 47–63). New York: Holt, Rinehart & Winston.

Castellano, K. E. and Ho, A. D. (2013). A practitioner's guide to growth models. *Council of Chief State School Officers*. Available at: www.

ccsso.org/Resources/Publications/A_Practitioners_Guide_to_Growth_Models.html. Accessed on June 8, 2015.

Center for Public Education (2007). *Measuring Student Growth: A guide to informed decision making.* Available at: www.centerforpublic education.org/Main-Menu/Policies/Measuring-student-growth-At-a-glance/Measuring-student-growth-A-guide-to-informed-decision-making.html. Accessed on November 2, 2015.

Costa, A.L. and Kallick, B. (2009). *Habits of Mind Across the Curriculum.* Alexandria, VA: ASCD.

Cotton, K. (1988). *Monitoring Student Learning in the Classroom.* School Improvement Research Series. Office of Educational Research and Information (OERI). U.S. Department of Education. Available at: http://educationnorthwest.org/sites/default/files/Monitoring StudentLearning.pdf. Accessed on October 22, 2014.

Council for the Accreditation of Teacher Preparation. Available at: http://caepnet.org. Accessed on January 4, 2016.

Council of Chief State School Officers (CCSSO) (2012). *Distinguishing Formative Assessment from Other Educational Assessment Labels.* Prepared by FAST/SCASS. Available at: www.ccsso.org/Resources/Publications/Distinguishing_Formative_Assessment_from_Other_Educational_Assessment_Labels.html. Accessed on November 16, 2014.

Covey, S. (1998). *7 Habits of Highly Effective Teens.* New York: Touchstone.

Csikszentmihalyi, M. (2008). *Flow: The Psychology of Optimal Experience.* New York: Harper and Row.

Darling-Hammond, L. (2014). "Testing to, and Beyond, the Common Core: New assessments can support a multiple-measure framework to deepen teaching and learning." *Principal (NAESP),* January/February 2014, pp. 11–14.

Darling-Hammond, L., Herman, J., Pellegrino, J., Abedi, J., Aber, J.L., Baker, E., Bennett, R., Gordon, E., Haertel, E., Kakuta, K., Ho, A., Lee Linn, R., Pearson, P.D., Popham, J., Resnick, L., Schoenfeld, A.H., Shavelson, R., Shepard, L.A., Shulman, L., and Steele, C.M. (2013). *Criteria for High-Quality Assessment.* SCOPE, CRESST, and Learning Sciences Research Institute. Available at: https://edpolicy.stanford.edu/publications/pubs/847. Accessed in April 2014.

Donoso, M., Collins, A.G.E., and Koechlin, E. (2014). "Human Cognition. Foundations of Human Reasoning in the Prefrontal Cortex." *Science*, 344 (6191), pp. 1481–1486.

Dweck, C. (2008). *Mindset: The new psychology of success*. New York: Random House/Ballantine.

Eberley Center for Teaching Excellence and Educational Innovation. Available at: www.cmu.edu/teaching/assessment/howto/basics/objectives.html. Accessed in June 2015.

Egbert, M.D. and Barandiaran, X.E. (2014). "Modeling Habits as Self-Sustaining Patterns of Sensorimotor Behavior." *Frontiers in Human Neuroscience*. Available at: http://journal.frontiersin.org/Journal/10.3389/fnhum.2014.00590/full. Accessed in August 2014.

Fisher, D. and Frey, N. (2008). "Releasing Responsibility." *Educational Leadership*, 66 (3), pp. 32–37.

Fisher, D. and Frey, N. (2013). *Better Learning Through Structured Teaching: A gradual release of responsibility* (2nd ed.). Alexandria, VA: ASCD.

Florida Department of Education (2011). *Recommendations of the Florida Student Growth Implementation Committee*. Available at: www.fldoe.org/teaching/performance-evaluation/student-growth.stml. Accessed on June 27, 2014.

Fuchs, L.S. and Fuchs, D. (2002). *Using CBM for Progress Monitoring*. Available at: www.studentprogress.org/library/training/cbm%20reading/usingcbmreading.pdf. Accessed on September 8, 2014.

Galan, C. (2015). *At the Heart*. Available at: http://blog.remind.com/author/clara/. Accessed on August 19, 2015.

Glossary of Education Reform. (2013). *Great School Partnership*. Available at: http://edglossary.org/learning-progression/. Accessed on August 25, 2014.

Goldman, D. (2010). "Gene x Environment Interactions in Complex Behavior: First build a telescope. Biological Psychiatry." *National Institutes of Health*, 67 (4), pp. 295–296.

Greenberg, J. and Walsh, K. (2012). *What Teacher Preparation Programs Teach About K-12 Assessment: A review of the research*. National Council on Teacher Quality. Available at: www.nctq.org/dms View/What_Teacher_Prep_Programs_Teach_K-12_Assessment_NCTQ_Report. Accessed on October 7, 2015.

Greenstein, L. (2010). *What Teachers Really Need to Know About Formative Assessment.* Alexandria, VA: ASCD.

Gyllander, L. (2013). Opportunities and Constrains Arise When Teachers and Students Attempt Developing a Reciprocal Assessment Practice Through Collaboration. *ECER Conference: Creativity and Innovation in Educational Research.* Available at: www.eera-ecer.de/ecer-programmes/pdf/conference/8/contribution/22592/. Accessed on January 9, 2015.

Hattie, J. (2009). *Visible Learning: A synthesis of over 800 meta-analyses relating to achievement.* New York: Routledge.

Hattie, J. (2011). *Visible Learning for Teachers.* New York: Routledge.

Hattie, J. and Timperley, H. (2007). The Power of Feedback. *Review of Educational Research,* 77 (81). AERA and SAGE Publications. Available at: http://education.qld.gov.au/staff/development/performance/resources/readings/power-feedback.pdf. Accessed on July 30, 2012.

Heritage, M. (2010). *Formative Assessment and Next-Generation Assessment Systems: Are we losing an opportunity?* University of California, CA: National Center for Research on Evaluation, Standards, and Student Testing (CRESST).

Hess, K. (2006). *Cognitive Complexity: Applying Webb DOK levels to Bloom's taxonomy.* Dover, NH: National Center for Assessment.

Hess, K. (2008). *Developing and Using Learning Progression as a Scheme for Measuring Progress.* National Center for Assessment. Available at: www.nciea.org/publications/CCSSO2_KH08.pdf. Accessed on May 6, 2014.

Joint Committee on Standards for Educational Evaluation. (2015). *Classroom Assessment Standards.* Available at: www.jcsee.org/the-classroom-assessment-standards-new-standards. Accessed on November 24, 2015.

Kahl, S.R. (2010). Something Old, Something New: What teachers as assessors must know and be able to do. *The Source.* Available at: www.advanc-ed.org/source/something-old-something-new-what-teachers-assessors-must-know-and-be-able-do. Accessed on August 25, 2014.

Kahl, S.R., Hofman, P., and Bryant, S. (2013). *Assessment Literacy Standards and Performance Measures for Teacher Candidates and Practicing Teachers.* Washington, DC: Council for the Accreditation of Educator Preparation (CAEP).

Karpicke, J.D. (2012). "Retrieval-Based Learning: Active retrieval promotes meaningful learning." *Association for Psychological Services: Current Directions in Psychological Services*, 221 (3), pp. 157–163.

Kellough, R.D. and Kellough, N.G. (1999). *Secondary School Teaching: A guide to methods and resources; Planning for competence.* Upper Saddle River, NJ: Prentice Hill.

Killian, S. (2015). 8 Strategies Robert Marzano and John Hattie Agree On. *The Australian Society of Evidence Based Teaching.* Available at: www.evidencebasedteaching.org.au/robert-marzano-vs-john-hattie/. Accessed on November 15, 2015.

Kierkegaard, Søren. *Journalen JJ*: 167 (1843), *Søren Kierkegaards Skrifter*, Søren Kierkegaard Research Center, Copenhagen, 1997–, volume 18, p. 306.

Kluger, A. and DeNisi, A. (1996). The Effects of Feedback Interventions on Performance: A historical review, a meta-analysis, and a preliminary feedback intervention theory. *American Psychological Association,* 119 (2), pp. 254–284. Available at: http://mario.gsia.cmu.edu/micro_2007/readings/feedback_effects_meta_analysis.pdf. Accessed on January 7, 2010.

La Marca, P.M. (2001). Alignment of Standards and Assessments as an Accountability Criterion. *Practical Assessment, Research & Evaluation,* 7 (21). Available at: http://PAREonline.net/getvn.asp?v=7&n=21. Accessed on February 7, 2009.

La Marca, P.M., Redfield, D., and Winter, P.C. (2000). *State Standards and State Assessment Systems: A guide to alignment.* Washington, DC: Council of Chief State School Officers.

McMillan, J.H. (2000). Fundamental Assessment Principles for Teachers and School Administrators. *Practical Assessment, Research, and Evaluation.* Available at: http://pareonline.net/getvn.asp?v=7&n=8. Accessed on August 19, 2007.

McMillan, J.H. (2011). *Classroom Assessment: Principles and practices for effective standards-based instruction.* New York: Pearson.

McMillan, J.H. and Hearn, J. (2008). Student Self-Assessment: The key to stronger student motivation and higher achievement. *Educational Horizons,* Fall 2008, pp. 40–48. Available at: http://files.eric.ed.gov/fulltext/EJ815370.pdf. Accessed on October 24, 2014.

Mansell, W. and James, M. (2009). *Assessment in Schools. Fit for Purpose?* London: Assessment Reform Group.

Marshall, B. and Drummond, M. J. (2006). How Teachers Engage with Assessment for Learning: Lessons from the classroom. *Research Papers in Education*, 21 (2), pp. 133–149.

Marzano, R. (2003). *What Works in Schools: Translating research into action*. Alexandria, VA: ASCD.

Marzano, R. (2007). *The Art and Science of Teaching*. Alexandria, VA: ASCD.

Mertler, C. (2009). Teachers' Assessment Knowledge and Their Impression of the Impact of Classroom Assessment Professional Development. *Improving Schools, 12* (2), pp. 101–113. Available at: http://imp.sagepub.com/content/12/2/101.abstract. Accessed on October 25, 2015.

Moon, J. (2005). *Linking Levels, Learning Outcomes and Assessment Criteria*. Exeter, UK: Exeter University.

National Center for Research on Evaluation, Standards, and Student Testing: CRESST. Available at: www.cse.ucla.edu/. Accessed on March 27, 2010.

National Center for the Improvement of Educational Assessment. Available at: www.nciea.org. Accessed on March 27, 2010.

National Council for Accreditation of Teacher Education. Available at: www.ncate.org. Accessed on March 22, 2010.

National Council of Teachers of English (2013). Formative Assessment that Truly Informs Instruction. NCTE Board of Directors. Available at: www.ncte.org/library/NCTEFiles/Resources/Positions/formative-assessment_single.pdf. Accessed on February 16, 2015.

National Council on Measurement in Education. Available at: www.ncme.org. Accessed on March 22, 2010.

National Governors Association Center for Best Practices, Council of Chief State School Officers (2010). Common Core State Standards. National Governors Association Center for Best Practices, Council of Chief State School Officers, Washington D.C.

National Research Council (2001). *Knowing What Students Know: The science and design of educational assessment*. Washington, DC: National Academy Press.

OECD/CERI (2008). *Assessment for Learning—-The case for formative assessment*. Paris: Organization for Economic Cooperation and Development. Available at: www.oecd.org/site/educeri21st/40600533.pdf. Accessed on March 22, 2010.

Oxford Dictionaries (2016). Oxford University Press. Available at: www.oxforddictionaries.com. Accessed on January 30, 2016.

Paris, S.G. and Paris, A.H. (2001). Classroom Applications of Research on Self-Regulated Learning. *Educational Psychologist*, 36 (2), pp. 89–101. Available at: http://lchc.ucsd.edu/MCA/Mail/xmca mail.2013_09.dir/pdf4cg5OwMfev.pdf. Accessed on October 9, 2010.

Patall, E.A., Cooper, H., and Robinson, C. (2008). "The Effect of Choice on Intrinsic Motivation and Related Outcomes: A meta-analysis of research findings." *Psychological Bulletin*, 134 (2), pp. 280–300.

PBS Newshour Extra (2013). *The Science of Stress: How well do you test?* Available at: www.pbs.org/newshour/extra/2013/02/the-science-of-stress-how-well-do-you-test/. Accessed on October 23, 2014.

Pellegrino, J. and Hilton, M. (Eds.) (2012). *Education for Life and Work: Developing transferrable skills in the 21st century*. Washington, DC: National Academies Press.

Peter, L. (1977). *Peter's quotations*. New York: HarperCollins.

Pink, D. (2011). *Drive: The surprising truth about what motivates us*. New York: Penguin.

Popham, J.W. (2008). *Transformative Assessment*. Alexandria, VA: ASCD.

Rand Education (2012). *Teachers Matter: Understanding teacher's impact on student achievement*. Available at: www.rand.org/pubs/cor porate_pubs/CP693z1-2012-09.html. Accessed on May 2, 2014.

Sanders J.R. (Chair) (2000). *Standards for Teacher Competence in Educational Assessment of Students*. Washington, DC: American Federation of Teachers, National Council on Measurement in Education, National Education Association.

Schwartz, D.L. and Arena, D. (2013). *Measuring What Matters Most*. Cambridge, MA: MacArthur Foundation, MIT Press.

Scriven, M. (1967). "The Methodology of Evaluation." In R.W. Tyler, R.M. Gagne, and M. Scriven (Eds.), *Perspectives of Curriculum Evaluation* (pp. 39–83). Chicago, IL: Rand McNally.

Shepard, L.A. (2000). *The Role of Classroom Assessment in Teaching and Learning*. National Center for Research on Evaluation, Standards, and Student Testing. CRESST, University of Colorado at Boulder. Available at: www.cse.ucla.edu/products/reports/TECH517.pdf. Accessed on May 2, 2014.

Shepard, L.A. (2005). "Linking Formative Assessment to Scaffolding." *Educational Leadership*, 63 (3), pp. 68–73.

Shute, V. (2007). *Focus on Formative Feedback*. Princeton, NJ: ETS. Available at: www.ets.org/Media/Research/pdf/RR-07-11.pdf. Accessed on December 1, 2014.

Stanford, P., Crowe, M.W., and Flice, H. (2010). "Differentiating with Technology." *Teaching Exceptional Children Plus*, 6 (4), Article 2. Available at: http://files.eric.ed.gov/fulltext/EJ907030.pdf. Accessed on April 17, 2014.

Stiggins, R. (2005). "From Formative Assessment to Assessment for Learning." *Phi Delta Kappan*, 87 (4), pp. 324–328.

Suskie, L. (2000). "Fair Assessment Practices." *AAHE Bulletin*, 14. Available at: http://uncw.edu/cas/documents/FairAssessment Practices_Suskie.pdf. Accessed on December 1, 2014.

Thorndike, E. (1911). *Animal Intelligence: Experimental studies*. New York: Transaction Publishers.

Tomlinson, C. and Moon, T. (2013). *Assessment and Student Success in a Differentiated Classroom*. Alexandria, VA: ASCD.

Vander Ark, T. and Schneider, C. (2012). *Deeper Learning for Every Student Every Day*. GettingSmart.com and The William and Flora Hewlett Foundation. Available at: www.hewlett.org/sites/ default/files/Deeper Learning for Every Student Every Day, GETTING SMART_1.2014.pdf. Accessed on January 3, 2016.

Webb, N. (1997). *Web Alignment Tool*. University of Wisconsin, Madison, WI: Wisconsin Center of Educational Research.

Wiggins, G. (2014). Validity, Part 1 (revised). Available at: https:// grantwiggins.wordpress.com/2014/02/20/validity-part-1-revised/. Accessed on January 3, 2016.

Wiggins, G. and McTighe, J. (2005). *Understanding by Design* (2nd ed.). Alexandria, VA: ASCD.

Wiliam, D. (2011). *Embedded Formative Assessment*. Bloomington, IN: Solution Tree.

Willis, J. (2014a). *The Neuroscience Science Behind Stress and Learning*. Available at: www.edutopia.org/blog/neuroscience-behind-stress-and-learning-judy-willis. Accessed on November 23, 2014.

Willis, J. (2014b). *5 Assessment Forms That Promote Content Retention*. Edutopia. Available at: www.edutopia.org/blog/assessment-forms-promote-content-retention-judy-willis. Accessed on November 23, 2014.

Wilson, M. and Sloane, K. (2000). "From Principles to Practice: An embedded assessment system." *Applied Measurement in Education*, 13, pp. 181–208. Available at: http://dev.valdosta.edu/academics/general-education-council/documents/principles toprac.pdf. Accessed on March 25, 2014.

Woytek, A. (2007). *Utilizing Assessment to Improve Student Motivation and Success*. University of South Carolina, Aiken, SC: Essays in Education.

Author Index

Subject Index

CPSIA information can be obtained
at www.ICGtesting.com
Printed in the USA
FFHW020531291118
49683569-54061FF